T0277293

# Cambridge Elements ≡

**Elements in Critical Heritage Studies**
edited by
Kristian Kristiansen, *University of Gothenburg*
Michael Rowlands, *UCL*
Francis Nyamnjoh, *University of Cape Town*
Astrid Swenson, *Bath University*
Shu-Li Wang, *Academia Sinica*
Ola Wetterberg, *University of Gothenburg*

# CONSTRUING CULTURAL HERITAGE: THE STAGINGS OF AN ARTIST

## *The Case of Ivar Arosenius*

Mats Malm

*University of Gothenburg*

CAMBRIDGE
UNIVERSITY PRESS

# CAMBRIDGE
## UNIVERSITY PRESS

University Printing House, Cambridge CB2 8BS, United Kingdom

One Liberty Plaza, 20th Floor, New York, NY 10006, USA

477 Williamstown Road, Port Melbourne, VIC 3207, Australia

314–321, 3rd Floor, Plot 3, Splendor Forum, Jasola District Centre,
New Delhi – 110025, India

79 Anson Road, #06–04/06, Singapore 079906

Cambridge University Press is part of the University of Cambridge.

It furthers the University's mission by disseminating knowledge in the pursuit of
education, learning, and research at the highest international levels of excellence.

www.cambridge.org
Information on this title: www.cambridge.org/9781108794503
DOI: 10.1017/9781108885652

© Mats Malm 2021

First published 2021

*A catalogue record for this publication is available from the British Library.*

ISBN 978-1-108-79450-3 Paperback
ISSN 2632-7074 (online)
ISSN 2632-7066 (print)

Additional resources for this publication at www.cambridge.org/malm

# Construing Cultural Heritage: The Stagings of an Artist

## The Case of Ivar Arosenius

Elements in Critical Heritage Studies

DOI: 10.1017/9781108885652
First published online: May 2021

Mats Malm
*University of Gothenburg*

**Author for correspondence:** Mats Malm, mats.malm@lir.gu.se

**Abstract:** This study examines how an artist construed himself as cultural heritage by the turn of the nineteenth century, how this heritage was further construed after his death and how the artworks can be made to further new approaches and insights through a digital archive (aroseniusarkivet.dh.gu.se). The study employs the concept of 'staging' to capture the means used by the artist, as well as by reception, in this construal. The question of 'staging' involves not only how the artist has been called forth from the archives, but also how the artist can be called forth in new ways today through digitization. The study first elaborates on the theoretical framework through the aspects of mediation and agency, then explores how the artist was staged after his death. Finally, the artist's own means of staging himself are explored. Swedish painter Ivar Arosenius (1878–1909) is the case studied.

**Keywords:** cultural heritage, staging, archive, reception, media

ISBNs:9781108794503 (PB), 9781108885652 (OC)
ISSNs:2632-7074 (online), 2632-7066 (print)

# Contents

This Element contains a number of images, but refers to many more. For a fuller experience the reader is advised to download the file with all images in colour and have it alongside while reading: aroseniusarkivet.dh.gu.se/construing.pdf and also available at www.cambridge.org/malm. At aroseniusarkivet.dh.gu.se, the reader will also be presented with a wealth of material for further exploration.

This study was written as part of a project funded by The Royal Swedish Academy of Letters, History and Antiquities and Riksbankens Jubileumsfond.

# 1 Introduction

Ivar Arosenius holds a very special position in Swedish art history. His paintings often tell a striking story in a highly idiosyncratic yet remarkably universal vocabulary. Their impact on the viewer is at many times considerable, largely but not only because of their forceful imagination. Arosenius' reputation as a painter largely rests on his innovative relation to tradition, but the more or less cultic attention to him is due not only to the enigmatic character of many of his paintings, but also to the fact that he died very young, only thirty years old, from haemophilia. Born in 1878, he passed away on New Year's Day 1909.

The particular circumstances surrounding Arosenius illustrate the impossibility of understanding an artist and his or her position without examining how the artist has been treated and construed in reception up to the present day. The moulding of this cultural heritage takes place in different waves and stages, through exhibitions, reviews, studies, etc., gradually forming the complex image of today. In order to better understand this example of cultural heritage as it meets us, we need to study how it was construed. It is, however, not merely a question of reception history, since the artist can be assumed to have wished to establish him/herself as, precisely, cultural heritage. So, for a fuller understanding, there is also a need to examine how the artist attempted to construe him/herself.

Reception is very much the process that produces cultural heritage, but it is also a very broad phenomenon. In order to make it manageable, in this context I will limit the inquiry to *stagings*: cases of reception where a scholar, curator, writer or the like has presented the artist from a certain understanding and from a particular selection of works. This staging of the artist from the archives obviously stresses some aspects and ignores others. Staging is not the same as reception: it is active and mediating, performed by curators, authors and the like, rather than the more personal and, usually, unstructured reception of audiences in general. The concept of staging, however, is not restricted to reception. It proves useful also for studying how the artist endeavoured to construe his or her own persona and position; staging him/herself mainly through the works of art, although interviews and manifests, for example, would be additional means of self-staging.[1] The stagings of the artist and those of posterity sometimes coincide in ambition, and sometimes deviate considerably from each other, in their evolution into the cultural heritage we meet.

---

[1] The concept of staging connects to performance, but the performativity is here not that of the scene. Rather, it connects to J. L. Austin's speech act theory (Austin 1962). Strictly speaking, 'illocutionary' must apply to language, but through the stagings of the artist, the work of art very distinctly addresses its receiver and effects notions if not actions.

The artist's staging him/herself can be seen as part of an effort to establish a public persona and thus to make him/herself into cultural heritage. This staging is for natural reasons less concise than the one performed by a scholar, curator or writer. It has taken place over a number of years and changed for a number of reasons, and it has been presented largely through the works of art, which have since been scattered to a number of different places. So: how to trace the stagings of the artist? The Arosenius Archive (aroseniusarkivet.dh.gu.se) is a case study which proposes to provide the means for such examinations by collecting the artist's works from various archives – primarily museums such as the Gothenburg Museum of Art and the Swedish National Museum, as well as the artist's notes, sketches, letters, photographs, etc. from the Gothenburg University Library where they are deposited – and private owners.

The works and sources are collected digitally, and offered to all users for free consideration. A number of tools are offered for structuring, filtering and understanding the works of the artist in ways that have not previously been possible – or for critically tracing and examining previous understandings, with the aid of a much larger body of material than they could embrace. That is, the Arosenius Archive stages the artist anew, offering the public as well as researchers the opportunity once again to stage the artist according to any aspects they wish to pursue – or, simply, to approach the artist bypassing established historical prejudice. The ambition is to let the artefacts speak for themselves, alone or in conjunction, through contexts new and old. The artefacts include a number of different kinds of objects, not only what would traditionally be described as artworks: the distinction between works of art and other objects is sometimes a useful simplification, but the combination of kinds is intended to, in the end, enable disregarding of such borders. Thus, the intention is to enable new kinds of exchange between the audience/users and the artist.

The present study is devoted to three different instances of staging the artist Ivar Arosenius. Section 2 constitutes a discussion of the different ways an artist or a collection may be called forth from the archives and staged through digital media. The theoretical foundations and framework will be clarified through the aspects of mediation and agency.

Section 3 examines how the artist was staged after his death, in monographs and anthologies. The admittedly important newspaper reviews are for practical reasons left to future research, while the corpus here treated consists in more 'long-lasting' and elaborate stagings, more readily available to readers over long periods of time (the entries on Arosenius in works of art history are often written by the same authors, and are not brought into discussion as they do not add substantially to the picture of the artist). Arosenius' real breakthrough came with an exhibition a little more than a month before his death, and the intention is to clarify the different attempts to establish the artist as cultural heritage.

Section 4 is devoted to an attempt that can be phrased in two ways: it may be seen as an analysis of how the artist staged himself in and through his art, directing how to be understood and steering the subsequent collecting, archiving and presentations of his works. It may also be seen not as focused on the artist's intentions, but attempting to let the artefacts themselves speak, tracing how the artist emerged through them. The concept of staging is applied to the artefacts in different ways that structure the examination, in the end illuminating not only how the artist's role and character were devised, but also how he staged his home, his family and himself as viewed and viewer, and in the end how he staged the beholder of his paintings.

Section 4 utilizes the Arosenius Archive not so much with regard to tools as with regard to collected resources: it employs the aggregation of artefacts, works, drafts, etc. into an archive more comprehensive than anyone has previously had access to. The analysis thus takes its point of departure from the Arosenius Archive; so, too, does the form of presentation, utilizing the medium in an exploratory fashion. In this section, frequent reference will be made to various works of art. This Element contains a limited set of illustrations, but as more images are essential for a fuller understanding, the Element should be read together with the wider selection of images available at aroseniusarkivet.dh.gu.se/construing.pdf. Thus, the figures referred to in this study are consecutively numbered, but not all of them are rendered here as images – they are all found in the PDF file at the web address.

The ambition is to enter a future path of studying the artefacts detached from their usual context and thus to an extent letting the artefacts structure our understanding, on the one hand as they create the scene for themselves and the artist, and on the other hand as they work – individually and collectively – to orchestrate the reactions and reception of the audience. The options for releasing the artefacts will be more numerous and powerful in the future, as, for instance, works may be mapped against other works on the Internet, allowing connections, coincidences and influences to emerge. It will then also be possible to relate them to other, larger patterns and narratives, such as those of artistic periods and general developments. This is to be understood as a first, tentative attempt at mapping possibilities and options.

## 2 The Work of Art and the Archive

### 2.1 Mediation

What does digitization do to works of art, to artists and to the archives? It may be illuminating to start thinking of this age of constantly accelerating reproduction in the light of a previous technological revolution – that of photography. Walter Benjamin in his famous 1935 article 'The Work of Art in the Age of Mechanical Reproduction' proposed that the photographic reproduction not only lacked the (not so easily defined) *aura* of the original work of art, but also diminished the aura of the original: 'that which withers in the age of mechanical reproduction is the aura of the work of art'.[2] This description would invite us to understand the work of art as being all the more extenuated and flattened in our own, very much more efficient, age of digital reproduction.

However, at the same time, Benjamin underscored that the reproduction 'enables the original to meet the beholder halfway' (Benjamin 1968, 220). And as has been demonstrated by Peter Walsh (2007), the truth of the aura seems to be quite the opposite. Photographic reproduction did not destroy the aura of the work of art; rather, it created it. Walsh builds his argument on the development of museums: what he calls 'pre-photographic museums' were built around collections of original works of art which had in different ways ended up in a place for exhibiting. The ambition of the museums was not to represent art and art history as such, but merely the collection in question. Around 1800, they were not rarely expanded into monuments of the nation, region or other powers and institutions.

From the middle of the nineteenth century, photography caused the emergence of the 'post-photographic' museum, which was not dedicated to a collection but could instead aim at presenting great art and art history. These museums, exemplified by Walsh with South Kensington Museum (today's Victoria and Albert), would use originals, casts, copies and photographs without actual discrimination. In effect, photographs were in some cases significantly more powerful than originals. Through the photographs, hierarchies were changed: less accessible works of art could be made known and be attributed a place in art history, and a distinct effect of photography and publication was the canonization of that which was most readily disseminated. As certain paintings were more suited for black-and-white photography, even colour scales could and would change an object's place in the hierarchy.

Simultaneously, photographic reproductions established new practices for the exhibiting of originals. Previously, works of art had been improved in

---

[2] Quoted from Benjamin 1968, 221.

different ways: missing parts of sculptures had been filled out, paintings had been retouched and adapted – but photography introduced a view of the original in its current state, documenting flaws and wear rather than reconstructing a posited ideal.[3] Thus developed the practice in museums to exhibit originals without 'improving' them, but rather viewing damage now as an important sign of their age, originality and authenticity.

Thus, even as the post-photographic museum replaced photographs and other reproductions with originals in their galleries, the direct influence of photography lingered in the displays. Photographs had, ironically, made the originals themselves so important and valuable that curators could no longer tolerate anything less. The replacement of restoration for conservation had significant consequences:

> It is … the re-production that confers status and importance on the original. The more reproduced an artwork is – and the more mechanical and impersonal the reproductions – the more important the original becomes. … Even the massive, symbol-laden architecture of the post-photographic museum reflects this transformation of art from precious objects into sacred icons of deep quasi-religious power – all thanks to this power of photographic reproduction. (Walsh 2007, 28–30)

Thus, there is reason to argue that the work of art does not lose aura from mechanical reproduction, but rather the contrary. It is clear that the aura will be deeply affected by digitization. Walsh points at some effects: one is the increased awareness that photographic or digital reproductions are never neutral; another is that collecting, sharing and interpreting works of art is now possible for very many actors outside of museums and academia. Walsh concludes that while museums are entering the Web, considerable development remains.

As Walsh wrote this in 2007, much has taken place since, and the speed has increased significantly. This is not the place for an account of that development, but particular aspects should be commented on. The definition and understanding of cultural heritage as a rule varies for a number of reasons, but the fundamental reason is arguably mediation. Focusing on digitization from the perspective of photography's impact, the main points are the following:

• Photography instigated a number of processes and notions about the work of art, which developed over time and according to circumstances in unpredictable ways, exemplified by Benjamin's concept of the aura – which would with time be understood in the exact opposite manner, as Walsh shows.

---

[3] In terms less focused on media, Bennett's account of the development of the modern museum can be seen as the foundation of this view (Bennett 1995). Cf. Liepe 2018, 18–19.

Digitization has started a wealth of processes in considerably more foundational layers of society, with effects that are only gradually becoming visible.

• Photography sharpened the focus on the historicity and authenticity of the
items contained in the archive: reproductions enhanced our attention to the
original and authenticity. Analogously, digitization sharpens the focus on
the original in a number of ways – most obviously perhaps in the considerable
progress of book history, paradoxically through ethereal, digital reproductions causing decisive attention to the material dimensions of texts and their
impact on meaning and understanding. The existence of copies and the
possibilities of manipulating them further enhance the attention to the
original.

• Photography brought about new ways of handling and distributing artefacts,
causing new models of evaluation and understanding. Digitization provides
exponentially more means of handling and distributing, thus providing new
evaluations – both richer access to highly valued pieces of cultural heritage
and a redistribution of value hierarchies. As regards understanding, re-
contextualization on different levels, alignment and comparison provide
entirely new venues.

• Photography altered the notion of the archive: the collection of a museum
shifted significance from being its primary concern, to being part of a more
general exhibition, coupled with reproductions and introductions into wider
contexts and developments. Thus, photography also sharpened focus on the
archive, its degree of representativity, the ways into it and the manners for
staging its contents and artists. Digitization provides, among other things,
new ways to call forth, structure and filter the items of the archive, efficiently
re-contextualizing and merging them with larger materials in different ways.
The original will be less often actually brought out of the archive than before,
and will thus gain new status – the function of the physical archive as shrine
will be even more accentuated.

• Photography made art the property of everyone through reproductions.
Digitization not only adds pure reproduction, but also enhances the ways in
which reproductions may be handled and distributed. The visitor potentially
becomes a user, with swift access to substantial materials and collections
either provided at museums and other resources or distributed for gathering
and curating at one's own will, exhibiting (e.g. on a computer or television
screen), and examining for new patterns. Not only the ownership of art is
disseminated, but also the curatorship. The effect also applies to research and
other instances of interpretation: the materials will be available not only to
experts but to anyone, to stage, filter, contextualize and interpret in a number
of new ways, presenting materials and opinions in even more ways.

Accessibility through media thus to a great extent regulates hierarchies and canon. Digitization can be expected to significantly increase this development – a development that certainly offers not only possibilities, but also risks.

As the post-photographic museum changed access to and notions of art, original, archive, value and knowledge, so the post-digital museum has the potential to accentuate these changes through a practically inexhaustible array of options for enhancing experience and augmenting reality. That is, access to and understanding of cultural heritage to a great extent change as a result of medial change. These changed understandings also include the artist him/herself, which calls for considerations on the relation between work, biography and history.

While the example of the photographic museum is illustrative of the fundamental role of mediation, in a sense it is an understatement. As David Bolter and Richard Grusin persuasively claimed in 1999, there is nothing prior to mediation. Explicating *remediation* as 'the Mediation of Mediation', they concluded:

> The events of our mediated culture are constituted by combinations of subject, media, and objects, which do not exist in their segregated forms. Thus, there is nothing prior to or outside the act of mediation.

In order to arrive at this conclusion, Bolter and Grusin adapted the concept of *hybrid* from Bruno Latour's *We Have Never Been Modern* (1993):

> For Latour, the phenomena of contemporary technoscience consist of intersections or 'hybrids' of the human subject, language, and the external world of things, and these hybrids are as real as their constituents – in fact, in some sense they are more real because no constituent (subject, language, object) ever appears in its pure form, segregated from the other constituents. (Bolter and Grusin 1999, 57–59; see also Blackman 2016, 38)

The inevitable conclusion is that cultural heritage must be understood not only as an object of mediation – things and ideas to be presented – but also as a process of mediation. Cultural heritage is readily described as a powerful social process for understanding both the past and the present, negotiating a number of discourses into cultural practice (Smith 2006, 304; cf. Harvey 2008, 20). Besides the social processes on individual and collective levels, the original work of art comes into being in a form which includes not only the technology for mediation and presentation, but also arrangement, selection, interpretation, etc. Cultural heritage is a blend of objects, presentations and negotiations which constantly develops not only through ideology, politics and aesthetics, but also through media technologies. Heritage in the making is heritage in the mediation.

## 2.2 Agency

The discussion so far has pointed to the agency of media: as regards the impact of photography on the museum, the nature and effects of its agency are fairly clear; as regards the impact of digitization on the museum and other modes of exhibiting archives, the nature and effects of the digital media are not yet as clearly discernible. Within Actor-Network Theory, agency has been attributed to non-human actors as well as human actors. Concerning museums and museal practices, the focus has been on objects as mediators, as discussions have been directed towards indigenous heritage and the need to de-colonialize heritage collections and exhibitions. The key to exploring these kinds of agency has been formulated as the 'processes of categorization, classification, ordering, and governance of things and people' (Harrison 2013, 8, 18). Ethnological and archaeological practices are at the forefront in a way that is not obviously applicable to the issue of art museums, yet the archival and museal approach calls for consideration.

The processes that have led to the archives and museums will not be followed up in this particular study. What is seminal, though, is the results of categorization, classification, ordering and to some extent governance in the reception of the artist's works. In the context of ethnographic museums, Latour's example of an Amazon expedition has been used for illustration:

> The plants find themselves detached, separated, preserved, classified, and tagged. They are then reassembled, reunited, redistributed according to entirely new principles that depend on the researcher, on the discipline of botany, which has been standardized for many centuries, and on the institution that shelters them, but they no longer grow as they did in the forest. The botanist learns new things, and she is transformed accordingly, but the plants are transformed also. (Latour 1999, 39)

Quoting this passage, Bennett et al. add that even the origin of the plants is transformed by environmental management that results from the collecting of the specimens. On the one hand, then, the processes are influenced by one another and human as well as non-human actors are involved. On the other hand, the objects, the non-human actors, are helplessly relocated into new contexts, where the meaning they are assigned has only rarely been that of their origin, as, for example, they have been inserted in constructions of social and cultural development (Bennett et al. 2017, esp. 24–26). Still, regardless of whether the meaning assigned to them by their new context is consistent with their origin or not, they have the potential of transforming audience and research.

By definition, the agency of things is demarcated by how they are categorized, ordered and handled as the result of human actors' social theories (Grinell and Portin unpublished). Such social theories may be taken to include aesthetic presumptions that surround the handling of artistic artefacts. In addition, the element of chance is crucial: what arrives at different archives may have been more or less fortuitous. As the artefacts have arrived, they have then been ordered, categorized, interpreted, exhibited and stabilized or frozen according to theoretical frameworks, explicit or implicit.

Latour's words on plants are easily transferrable to works of art: collected, assembled, ordered, classified and perhaps exhibited according to a number of aesthetic and scholarly theories as well as practical considerations, they have ended up in archives and collections where their testimony has been substantially overlaid with interpretations or simply silenced, blurred and/or stabilized into new meanings, their statement being diminished or altered.

The post-colonial critique of museal practices thus concerns, on the one hand, the processes that led to the current state, and on the other the options for freeing the objects from the frameworks they have been inserted into and opening them up for their own agency, or at least clarifying, altering and expanding the frames for their agency. This to a great extent can be said to imply reconfiguring the contexts of the objects: 'reassembling the collection', as Harrison (2013) puts it, or, in the suggestion of Grinell and Portin, re-defining and re-modelling the museum into a re-presenting instance, diplomatically offering its objects for constant renegotiation (Grinell and Portin unpublished; cf. Bennett 2018, 205). While it is not entirely clear how this is to be achieved in practice in archaeological museums, principally, the more objects and audience can be freed from fixation and ordering, the better they may form alternative orders.

The basic issue of Actor-Network Theory as applied to ethnographic and archaeological museums is to make the objects speak: to change them from silent intermediaries to mediators which do exert agency. As Latour outlines ways of making objects 'talk, that is, to offer descriptions of themselves, to produce scripts of what they are making others – humans or non-humans – do', his discussion is strikingly similar to the general approach of media theory towards media: the objects constantly risk receding into the background, and their 'mode of action' is not as visible anymore. Through innovations, controversies, mistakes or clumsiness, accidents and so on, 'silent intermediaries become full-blown mediators' in Latour's Actor-Network Theory. The point of departure for media theory, turning towards media archaeology, is that media remain transparent, unnoticeable, until something – a medial revolution, or something less grandiose – makes us suddenly see them and find ways to explore their nature, impact, import and agency. This exploration may often be performed in a Foucauldian archaeological manner, distinctly reminiscent of Latour's suggestion that the objects can be brought back to light through a historical tracing of how 'machines, devices, and implements were born' (Latour 2005, 79–81; cf. Huhtamo and Parikka 2011 and Parikka 2013, 151). Applying this reasoning to artists and art, the works of art which have to a greater or lesser extent come to be fixated in their contexts can be called forth and presented anew in ways that make them talk of their origin, their context and some of the networks they arose in. Although conditions and effects differ, they can do this as originals or as reproductions.

The audience is a central actor not least as the receiver of the results of collecting and governing, ordering, interpreting and presenting. When Bolter and Grusin made the concept of remediation the foundation of long and wide debate and development, a seminal issue was how mediation and remediation destabilize the relation and interaction between domains such as the social, the psychological, the cultural and the aesthetic. Pointing to this and connecting to Latour's 'hybrid objects', Blackman underlines how the elusive boundaries between old and new media are paralleled by the relation between old and new audiences. Leaving the notion of cultural objects as fixed and finalized entities and focusing instead on the processes and interrelations between all actors, it is obvious that the new audience can take a more active part, being more in control of the objects in question (which, on the one hand, may liberate the audience from previous orders and thus acknowledge its agency, and on the other, subjects it to new orderings): 'In the context of digital media, audiences are now approached as potential co-producers of meaning and content' (Blackman 2016, 38). Still, the mechanisms of what Bolter and Grusin termed 'the double logic of *re*mediation' are complicated: on the one hand, there is a cultural logic dominated by the desire for transparent immediacy, effacing (the signs of) mediation; on the other hand, there is a cultural logic dominated by the fascination with media. The striving for immediacy, or presentness, Blackman argues, closely ties in with the issue of audience, curating and affect (Bolter and Grusin 1999, 21–44; Blackman 2016, 39–40).

We may conclude that digital representations and the way they are situated and contextualized provide a number of alternative venues for the conceptualization of artefacts, art, audience, affect, cognition, experience, power, archive, collection, exhibition, museum and knowledge production. The question is how to best make use of them: the options are manifold.

## 2.3 The Arosenius Archive

Principally, what a museum does may be described as stabilizing the artefact into a specific meaning (Guggenheim 2009, 44–45). The object becomes a quasi-object, a hybrid, the sum of all contributions by human and non-human actors: modifying it by selecting, ordering, interpreting and attributing meaning, de-contextualizing and re-contextualizing, weaving into new narratives, embedding and displaying in a particular surrounding with particular lighting, information, access, status and mediation (cf. Westin 2012, 20–23). The mediation of an artefact can, at least theoretically, be done without changing the message (by intermediaries), but as a rule, the message is changed, reshaped (by mediators). From that perspective, the goal must be to liberate the artefact from this stabilized state, allowing it to be interpreted anew by different actors in a process of constant interaction. One way of doing this is by illuminating the different networks and actors which lie behind what the visitor of a museum is presented with (Harrison et al. 2013; Bennett et al. 2017; Grinell and Portin unpublished; cf. Latour 2005, 247–249). The manner in which the Arosenius Archive works instead proceeds from the circumstance that the stabilization of objects is regularly achieved by isolating them (Guggenheim 2009, 45). Thus, the Arosenius Archive aims at de-isolating the objects, enabling them to form new constellations and contexts and make themselves heard from there.

Anthropological, or at least sociological, aspects could be applied to Arosenius' and other artists' work. Actor-Network Theory has been applied to artists such as Titian, in order to map the networks around distribution and acquisition of works of art (Rees Leahy 2009; cf. Latour 2005, 237). While the networks that created Arosenian collections and exhibitions are a significant issue within the Arosenius project, that aspect is at this stage only treated as regards select exhibitions, and even then with a focus on the artefacts rather than their history. Instead of tracing networks, the primary focus of the project is on creating new networks, in the wide sense of the term. The ambition is to set the artist's works in motion in a way that enables anyone not only to approach them according to a new network/context, but also to change focus, network and context.

We do not think that we are able to release the artefacts entirely, but we attempt a start. The translation of the artefacts into digital format in itself results in hybrids, and provides a new set of actors which, on the one hand, remove us further from the original and, on the other, in some ways bring us closer to and destabilize the object from previous layers of curation and interpretation. The digital image is one actor, and ensuing actors are the graphical interface as such, with different techniques for viewing, sorting, arranging, downloading and re-engaging by using the Application Programming Interfaces (APIs): all intended to give the user as much agency as possible in interpreting the objects – and give the objects as much agency as possible in expressing themselves in other ways than before. The metadata provided do not depart from the traditional, but are employed for ways of ordering and visualizing that very much deviate from the previous restrictions of the original artefacts. In addition, manners of sorting and viewing which do not depend on metadata are offered.

What, then, happens with the artefact's aura? We have seen Peter Walsh contradict Walter Benjamin by demonstrating that photography and other reproductions in fact increased or even gave rise to the artefact's aura, rather than diminishing it. Latour comes to a similar conclusion, although conditioned, regarding digital reproductions. Stating that 'Benjamin confused the notion of "mechanical reproduction" with the inequality in the techniques employed', Latour concludes that well-made reproductions may increase (and distribute) the aura of the original, while bad reproductions decrease the aura and in the end make the original vanish (Latour and Lowe 2011, esp. 283; cf. Silberman 2008).

In the Arosenius Archive, the digital reproductions are not of the kind Latour had in mind when exemplifying 'good reproduction'. The digital representations of the artefacts are as good as conditions allow, but not spectacular. Still, we believe that they will not diminish the aura of the originals, but rather increase it and extend it, disseminating them widely, putting them at the disposal of new groups in new ways. Simultaneously, the aura as well as the objects will undergo change, as they shift contexts and interpretational frames.

Obviously, works of art are in themselves mediations – of emotions, ideas, (apprehensions of) external reality, imaginations, relations, identities and so forth. When we speak of staging in the context of the artist, the artistic mediations as such can be seen as the artist's self-stagings, subsequently selected by others and presented according to a great number of parameters as new, varying stagings, which to different degrees depend on other kinds of mediation: journal print, reproductions, photographs and in the end digitizations. This span of levels of mediation opens for different ways of calling forth the artist from the archives, of staging him for new audiences. In this, the artworks themselves offer stagings of the artist, his family, his home and so on, governing the audience's notions not least of the artist himself.

The Arosenius project was active from 2016 to 2019, and comprised research as well as the building of a web portal which gathers the public collections of the artist's works together with a considerable number of privately owned artefacts and contents from the artist's archive deposited at Gothenburg University Library (aroseniusarkivet.dh.gu.se). By combining several archives and adding more and more new material, the drawback of digital representations – their lack of physicality – is turned into an asset. The ambition is to deliver the works from their physical contexts, instead re-ordering and re-contextualizing them in a number of different ways which to an extent must be governed by the assumptions embedded in the project, but with the aim of giving the users considerable freedom and independence in their own approaches. By releasing old arrangements and categorizations, the technical implementation is intended to give the artefacts the possibility of agency instead of simply conveying fixed meaning within the context in which they have previously been selected and ordered. Simultaneously, the users – the interested public as well as researchers – are afforded the agency of questioning traditionally attributed meaning, value and context to the artefacts. Developing tools for this will have to be done in stages, and the ideal will never be reached, but this is meant as a step towards exploring ways of liberating the agency of artworks and receivers – through the agency of media.

An archive such as this can never be complete, and it is by necessity filled with material which has been produced according to different methods, for different purposes and at different times. The basic sources are also of diverse kinds, gathered from different places. We certainly are aware that the project entails fixating objects into new categories, not least as every labelling of metadata constitutes an interpretative categorization. Still, the usefulness of metadata, for example for viewing everything pertaining to a specific year, place or person, is an indispensable asset for making it possible to re-order and re-contextualize the material in ways that transcend previous orderings and interpretations. We also develop methods for sorting and filtering objects without depending on metadata, through machine-learning methods that sort images according to likeness following a number of different parameters. These methods also have their restrictions and dangers – and there will be many more and much better methods in the future – but the more options the user has, the more freely the artefacts should be able to express themselves.

One of the fundamental categorizations when it comes to this kind of art is the biographical: just as theories of the social have been a driving force in the collecting and organizing of objects, theories of the individual, of art, of development and progress have also governed the understanding of art.[4] We cannot avoid biography – the archive does collect the oeuvre of a single artist – but we can offer the material outside of chronological and biographical struc-tures, and, particularly, outside of previous orderings, selections, exhibitions and interpretations. This is not to say that all of those previous constructions should be rejected, but only that they should be optional and presented as alternatives. The aim is to balance biographical aspects with a number of other aspects and options for approaching art and artist. In this, chronology is important even without biographical intents: for relating to other works,

---

[4] 'Things, quasi-objects, and attachments are the real center of the social world, not the agent, person, member, or participant – nor is it society or its avatars' (Latour 2005, 238).

sketches, annotations, etc. by the artist, and for contextualizing, ultimately, towards wider circles and art history.

In particular, the premise has very often been the notion of the artist's biography as a key to the artefacts and the artefacts as keys to his life, emotions, inner universe, and personal and artistic development. Development is a crucial factor also when the point of reference is art history. Still, following Latourian wordings (but obviously also a number of other theoretical developments), development in the sense of progress is a figure of thought that belongs to the metanarratives of the 'moderns'. As a result, it has been suggested that the definition of a museum should remove the current focus on 'society and its development' (Grinell and Portin unpublished). While that definition focuses on development in the society surrounding the museum, the concept of development deserves to be questioned also as it has governed understandings of societies in general and in particular, and as it has governed notions of art and artists, particularly since Romanticism and, indeed, the birth of the museum (cf. Bennett 1995). In the case of the Arosenius Archive, one of the questions is how the artefacts may function when they are not related to the artist's biography and inserted into the history of a soul.

Hopefully, the portal will supply future research with the foundations for exploring such questions as well as others. The works of Arosenius often have a strong emotional impact on the viewer – an impact that is weakened as they are ordered according to theoretical structures such as catalogues, scholarly studies and even exhibitions. The project hopes to be able to release each work of previous contexts, enabling the viewer to experience it alone, filling screen and attention in its own right.[5] To be sure, the affective impact will not be physical in the same way as experiencing a work of art in real, physical life. On the other hand, the experience will be comparatively undisturbed, and it will be possible to see the image at any scale – many of Arosenius' works are astoundingly minute when seen in real life, often less than 10 × 10 cm. It is difficult to fathom a work like that on a large museum wall, surrounded by other paintings – the screen enables other approaches, sizings and perspectives, at the same time as the portal must of course clarify the dimensions of the original. Additionally, the lack of physical dimension is much compensated for by the fact that physical exhibitions are rare and extremely selective: here, a multitude of artworks from a large number of sources present themselves to the viewer-visitor-researcher-user – and for the curator-to-be, as anyone can use the material in their own applications.

---

[5] This opens up for entirely work-immanent interpretation, which in a sense is a natural part of Latourian agency of the work of art. On the other hand, our main focus is on the combinability and re-ordering of structures and frames of interpretation.

That kind of affect-related agency is to be easily exchanged for another, more cognitive kind, where the works of Arosenius are allowed to instigate or govern new structurings and categorizations of Arosenius' art. We start out with this ambition by trying to create a kind of kaleidoscopic effect: the viewer can sort, filter and order the material according to a number of parameters. These parameters (so far) mainly consist in metadata, which are of course based on previous categorizations and practices, but the user will be able to re-order them at will and the aim is to use machine learning to let algorithms order the material according to structure, lines, colour, etc. instead of metadata. The method for structuring material of this kind will of course be substantially developed in the future, hopefully in ways that this archive can profit from.

The works of art are thus expected to be endowed with a measure of agency partly by being allowed to address the viewer with the least possible amount of external noise (including ready-made orders and categories) and partly by being allowed to appear in new constellations and combinations, suggesting new orders and categories for being understood. This agency transfers to the viewer/user of this digital exhibition, who will be able to change between immediacy and hypermediacy, approach the material in his/her own way, and read a number of studies but then proceed from them and establish new orders, categories, hierarchies and studies.

The portal is named the Arosenius Archive (aroseniusarkivet.dh.gu.se), although it is not physical, since it is meant to constitute an alternative to the physical archive. The basic principles of ordering are fairly traditional, as are the metadata. However, the difference from the ordinary archive is that the ordering principles can be rapidly changed and combined by the user in a number of ways. It is more complete than the archives and collections which it has gathered, and all objects are equally available. It corresponds not only to an archive but also to all exhibitions and other stagings for which an archive may be the basis – and the Arosenius Archive offers access to every single item in the archive at any time. Although it lacks materiality in the common sense, it should not be understood in Foucauldian terms as embodying the set of rules that restrict what can be said and thought ('embodying' rather than 'constitut-ing', as the material aspect of Foucault's 'archive' should not be forgotten: Bennett et al. 2017, 36). Although, obviously, it does contain restrictions, it is designed to offer a good number of possibilities and so provide a basis for future development of even more possibilities. In this way, the ambition is to offer an archive in the fundamental sense of the word, deriving from *arkhê*: beginning. The Arosenius Archive gathers, and provides, the starting-points.

While working with the construction of the portal, the project team has analysed the processes of digitization, re-constructed a selection of exhibitions in order to map how the artist has been staged historically and how the impact of exhibitions can be re-enacted, examined a number of separate publications on Arosenius up to the present in order to find out how the artist has been staged at different times, re-constructed the artist's home as his primary setting for self-representation and source for motifs, studied the artist's self-staging in his works, and explored a variety of means for distributing and enhancing the experience of and knowledge in the works.[6]

While a biographical interpretation risks making the artefacts passive intermediaries, the approach will hopefully to an extent be able to suggest ways of making them active mediators. This is a first try, based on the assumption that the construal of a portal such as the Arosenius Archive will prepare the ground for more fruitful, future approaches. The portal offers anyone interested a number of images, many of which have not been available before, and tools for ordering and approaching them in a number of ways. This, it is hoped, is a way to put the artefacts at the forefront, before the artist's biography and other narrative structures. Every single artefact, through its reproduction, becomes an actor insofar as it can provide the point of departure for zooming in on its (when existent) conception and drafts, its context, its chronological setting, its motif and structure – the latter tracing resemblance through the artist's works, and in a hopefully not too distant future also directing searches for similarity on the World Wide Web. In these ways, the artefact can lead the user – if the user allows – further to a great set of related material and insights.

This section, describing the theoretical and practical framework of the project, is followed by Section 3 on how Arosenius was staged after his death. The subsequent Section 4 of this study utilizes the merging of archives into a fuller collection of sources than has previously been available, and at the same time through the method for presentation of the analysis is also an exploration of the agency of things and media. The standard problem for art history is the material conditions of its objects: reproduction in books is expensive, and images need space in order to perform. This means that the researcher needs to be selective and cannot adduce all the examples and evidence that would have been pertinent. On the one hand, this restricts the possibilities to clarify and strengthen the argument; on the other, the works not reproduced may change owners and disappear out of sight, with not even a single reproduction of them to be found. This presentation takes advantage of the digital medium by offering a wider selection of works than the book can contain, making it possible to follow the argument closely through a downloaded file or on the Web.

---

[6]  Work that has so far been published is listed at aroseniusarkivet.dh.gu.se/forskning.

Hopefully, the argument will become more vivid and substantial – and hopefully, the immediate access to the archive will entice users to question or transcend the argument, ordering and interpreting the resources in new ways. This Element can be read on its own, but the path for increasing the experience begins at aroseniusarkivet.dh.gu.se/construing.pdf. The expanding website as such simultaneously provides contextualizing and contextualizable material.

## 3 The Artist and the Archive

While present-day notions of art, original and canon can partly be explained by the medial development as outlined in the previous section, notions of the artist and his/her relation to works, tradition, audience and value have of course evolved through the influence of a number of other factors. Artworks are subjected to direct kinds of mediation, but artists, appearing through a multitude of artworks, historical contexts and appreciations of life and social/historical circumstances, are mediated in additional, complex ways. The theories of individuality and biography are a set of social theories that tightly connect to art. Scholarly paradigms provide parallel, sometimes overlapping, discourses. Thus, as the artist, and not only the artworks, forms part of cultural heritage, a number of other processes interfere, all of which contribute to sequential constructions of the artist. These constructions may be seen as stagings of the artist from the archive, employing different materials in order to enhance different aspects and understandings of the artist. Ultimately, every interpretation may be seen as a staging (Rossholm Lagerlöf 2007, 60). In addition, the archive – physical or digital, literal or metaphorical – will necessarily comprise the artist's own stagings of him/herself: all those images and self-understandings that the artist strove to convey in building his/her position and public identity. This section will focus on the stagings of the artist by posterity; Section 4 will examine the artist's self-staging.

## 3.1 Biography and Life

The construal of artists in cultural historiography is regularly founded on substantially biographistic ambitions: seeing the artist through his/her works, and thus, in effect, ordering the works into a biographic narrative of the artist. The works of art can then even be interpreted as sources for the biography.[7] The biographical approach has, of course, wide ranges, from the ambition to understand an individual's inner life and emotions through all life's events, or

---

[7] On the development of the modern monograph's development in between oeuvre and biography from 1850 onwards, see Guercio 2006, esp. 148–180.

to map an imaginary universe, or to use one artist to represent an era, stage or culture, to creating a case study in order to map sociological and economic factors in cultural life – and a number of other approaches. The concept of *biographical fallacy* was coined even before discourse theory, and has provoked a number of controversies. The biographical approach has been much problematized and nuanced, but if there is anything at all that can with any certainty be maintained, it is that the borders between life, work and art are never possible to clearly define.[8] What is apparent is that artists have generally been called forth from the archives and staged in a number of different, very often biographistic, ways.

Tradition already offered a number of young dead artists and authors, whose abrupt ending of life and career instigated not only grief over what was lost through death, but also deep fascination with the tragic aspects of the artist's fate: Lord Byron and Vincent van Gogh are among the most renowned. We will return to the Vangoghian complex further on, but in order to establish the concept of 'aesthetically meaningful death', it may prove useful to start at another end.

As our case study Ivar Arosenius lived between 1878 and 1909, the reception of his work can be said to have started by the turn of the nineteenth century. Beginning with reviews, it continued with articles, books, exhibitions and exhibition catalogues. Scholarly and public interest of the time was substantially biographical, and this focus was much enhanced by Arosenius' penchant to introduce himself and his surroundings in his works, not to mention the fact that he died very young. Thus, his art was to a very great extent understood and interpreted from his biography, at the same time as his artworks were used as a source for his inner life. This approach was connected to notions of the artistic genius as obeying aesthetic demands rather than social conventions, and at the same time to positivist approaches according to which the aesthetically specific could be explained by the personally specific – the notion of an 'aesthetically meaningful life'.[9] This understanding of Arosenius is still strong, but it was extraordinarily forceful after his death, not only because of his medical condition, but also because he very much lived the model of the artistic bohemian and, in fact, to a high degree blended his life with his art.

The retrospective view of Arosenius has focused so much on his medical condition that we may speak of the main figure of thought in reception as 'the aesthetically meaningful death'. The expression was coined by Åsa Arping

---

[8] Prominent contributions to the debate have been Epstein (ed, 1991), Soussloff (1997) and Codell (2003).

[9] The phrase 'aesthetically meaningful life' was applied to literary studies by Thomas Olsson, connecting mainly to Peter Bürger (Olsson 1989).

(2014) in discussing the 1888 suicide of Swedish author Victoria Benedictsson and her afterlife in reception. This had been interpreted in the light of Elizabeth Bronfen's *Over Her Dead Body* (1992): the male fascination with the dead woman as dominating the understanding and reception of an artist/author (Larsson 2008). In the case of Benedictsson, it has been demonstrated that the woman author did not receive much acclaim for her writing as such after her death, but instead attracted substantial interest in her capacity as dead woman author, aestheticizing death. The notion of an aesthetically meaningful death was also incorporated by Benedictsson herself. It has been described as her own 'double view': the double exposure of women of what they are and what they could be (Lundbo Levy 1980, inspired by Bovenschen 1976). This entails a polarizing between feebleness and strength, illness and health, victim and heroine. That is: Benedictsson's writing was highly performative, establishing an understanding which would strengthen her post-mortem reception in terms of the aesthetically meaningful death. As Arping details the constituents of the 'aesthetically meaningful death', based on the male gaze on the dead female body, they are remarkably similar to those of Arosenius, despite their being modelled on dead females.

In very similar vein, Arosenius' reception has been dominated by dichotomies such as feebleness–strength, illness–health, victim–conqueror/challenger, femininity–masculinity and a life on the verge of death. The exploration of these dichotomies traditionally appears to have been the concern of women artists rather than male ones. Arosenius had himself to a great extent prepared for this understanding through his extraordinary kind of self-staging, a highly performative kind of work. Still, the focus on Arosenius' life and death did not diminish the focus on his works in the same way as befell the female authors, but it laid the ground for a substantial approach to his works as tokens of the aesthetically meaningful death. This aesthetically meaningful death may have been prepared by Arosenius himself, but it was developed into something very different in the post-mortem stagings.

## 3.2 Staging the Artist

The main monographs and chapters in anthologies since the death of Arosenius all constitute new stagings of the artist from the archive, each accomplished from its own ideological, scholarly and practical circumstances. That development is the topic of the following subsections.

The first book on Arosenius was published in the year of his demise: *Ivar Arosenius: Twenty-Nine Colour Pictures* (*Ivar Arosenius: Tjugonio bilder i färg*), 1909. It was a short introduction, accompanied by twenty-nine colour reproductions, published by Axel Romdahl, curator at the Art Department of the Gothenburg City Museum. Romdahl starts by establishing the image of the heritage of Arosenius as a shrine: 'Picture an old altar painting, where holy men and women move about in a motley throng of wretched, common and ordinarily insignificant people' (5). After dwelling on the metaphysical sanctity, purity and suffering of these holy, as it were haloed, persons, Romdahl concludes that they in his own day go by the name of genius (*snille*). Romdahl's first definition of a genius is that s/he was attributed happiness and suffering in equal measure; a definition fully filled by Arosenius. The notion of the aesthetically meaningful death becomes an interpretative and explanatory model which covers Arosenius' life from childhood on. Arosenius' disease is described as an estranging confinement, and the image 'strange bird' suggests the modernist image of the artist as derived from Baudelaire's 'L'Albatros' (first published in 1861). However, frequent metaphors suggesting growth and fertility point more towards romantic notions of the artist. Describing 'evolution' as a modern idol, Romdahl claims that Arosenius' development was independent of external impulses (11). Individuality and personal pain become the explanatory factor: the Paris works are presented as the result of haunted anxiety and a genius close to perdition (12). Romdahl divides the artist's life into three periods: the starting years, the time in Paris and the artist's fruition (and imminent end). This narrative comes close to Aristotle's division of the drama in three parts in the *Poetics*, and the period in Paris (1904–5) takes a place very close to the drama's *peripeteia*, the turn of the story into the inescapable end.

The first substantial book on Arosenius, *Ivar Arosenius*, was published in 1928 by Karl Asplund. His explicit intention was to collect and present oral and written information from persons and documents, combining them with more common knowledge into an 'intimate image of the human being'. Like Romdahl, he describes Arosenius as a genius, far removed from common people, and even reuses the image of the 'strange bird', adding strong organic metaphors and proposing that the 'cult' of Arosenius is both reasonable and legitimate (v–vi). Asplund develops Romdahl's description of secluded youth, suggesting here the foundation of a strong streak of bitterness in the artist, and declares Arosenius' bohemian lifestyle as an attempt to soothe anxiety about the disease and prospect of a premature death (10). Asplund is more open to actual influence than Romdahl, even though he states that Arosenius' personality 'burned through' all exterior influences (vii). As Asplund's project gives much more space for actual life-writing, the influence of literature takes on an important explanatory part.

While Asplund enumerates a number of sources for his book, including letters and other writings of Arosenius, he forcefully exploits Arosenius' paintings as a foundational source. His penetration of the artist's inner life – reconstruction of a soul's history – is regularly founded on a variety of paintings, which are said to clearly reflect the personal emotions and fantasies of Arosenius (e.g. 63–88). Some paintings, in fact, are 'personal emotional outbursts' and Arosenius' reading is used in the same way to hypothesize about his emotions and identification points. The second part of Asplund's book treats 'some traits in the art of Arosenius' (129–241). Here Asplund starts with a few pages on technique and material (131–135), but soon leaves the formal aspects for content: ideas and motifs. The key to this approach is the notion of Arosenius as a 'painter-poet' (målarpoet).

Much attention is devoted to Arosenius' relation to reality, and his contempt for formal and traditional methods as well as for realistic representation. Paintings of nature, portraits, Bacchus drinking, Venus/sexuality/love, comic drawings, and the dichotomy of good and bad are treated before Asplund turns to Lillan, Arosenius' daughter who took such a dominant place in the last, familial period of Arosenius' art. Asplund shows that Arosenius was keen to write, but never found a way to express in words what he so aptly and easily expressed in images (vii). This side of Arosenius paves the way for examining the narrative aspect of his paintings, especially the late fairy-tale series which conclude the examination. Some seminal influences are traced through Arosenius' reading, which again adds a source to the artist's imaginary universe.

In a small book named *Ivar Arosenius* from 1944, Axel Romdahl published a brief introduction to the artist, followed by thirty-one reproductions. Stressing the combinations of humour and seriousness, illusion and reality, he exemplified the double exposure of paintings which present exotic places but are based on specific locations in Gothenburg, and described Arosenius as the dreamer, although a dreamer fully aware of the force of reality. As Romdahl states, Arosenius only rarely wrote text to his fairy-tale series, and these texts never really added to the images (8). Yet, Romdahl presents the fairy-tale series as well as literary sketches by Arosenius, adding to them images with the same theme, but not necessarily intended by Arosenius to go together with the text. In addition, Romdahl presents a number of fairy-tale series that Arosenius did not attach text to – instead, we are presented with Romdahl's own texts to Arosenius' images.

Asplund's 1928 documentation of sources was supplemented three decades later by a book devoted to *Images of Recollection* (*Minnesbilder*), where two essays are on Arosenius. Arosenius' friend Signe Lagerlöw-Sandell adds substantial information not least about Arosenius' schooling in Gothenburg and the coterie around him. Describing the group's reading and discussions, she provided more details about Arosenius' reading and favourites, as well as about his remarkable memory. Ernst Spolén describes his and Arosenius' stay in Värmland in the summer of 1902, and the development Arosenius underwent there – meeting nature and country in a new way. He briefly describes visits to obscure bars and 'high life', something that, according to Arosenius, a physician had recommended him as a remedy for his haemophilia.

Besides the documentary information, the book presents a number of pictures that had not been published before: on the one hand, several of Arosenius' portraits of friends and sceneries not least from the early bohemian years; on the other hand, paintings he composed in Värmland. A large section of the book renders works by Arosenius which are not connected to the two essays, but open up his imaginary universe, accompanied by quotations and commentaries from a number of reviews and other sources. The images presented in connection with Lagerlöw-Sandell's essay to a great extent consist of Arosenius' portraits and pictures of himself and his friends or surroundings, and significantly add to the impression of Arosenius as an artist who very much turned his everyday life into art.

In 1944, Romdahl had characterized Arosenius as very different from the introvert and unwieldy Swedish national character (5). In *Images of Recollection*, Spolén places him in the middle of Swedish rural life, underscoring how much at home he felt there compared to the city, and in the section of paintings, several statements from reviews, etc. describe Arosenius in nationalistic terms. Not only the paintings that induce these quotations are of the kind that may convey a sense of Swedish nature and nationality, but also several more of the works reproduced in this volume.

An exhibition at the Gothenburg Museum of Art in 1958–9 was accompanied by a publication called, not surprisingly, *Ivar Arosenius. 1879–1909*. There, the art historian Sven Sandström offered a short presentation of the artist. Sandström starts with Arosenius' will to provoke laughter, and underlines the intensity of his emotional life by explaining his art not only by his father's death but, more significantly, with the afflicting end of his relationship with Ester Sahlin, which is here described as causing an extreme reaction, immediately reflected in his art and resulting in 'some of the most fierce and painful diatribes in Swedish art' (12). Sandström also describes the late fairy-tale series as a culmination of the art of the time, a uniquely genuine contribution (18).

In recognition of the fiftieth anniversary of Arosenius' death in 1959, a popular Christmas issue in large format but with few pages, *Christmas Spirit (Julstämning)*, was published. It presented a good deal of colour reproductions, a brief essay by Sandström and a short text by Arosenius' widow, Eva Arosenius. In a way reminiscent of Romdahl, Sandström presented Arosenius as the great storyteller, characterized by his ability to create fairy-tales in images in need of no text. The essay is followed by two of Arosenius' fairy-tale series – both accompanied by the textual paraphrases composed by Axel Romdahl in 1939. Sandström iterates the view of Arosenius' paintings (after the break with Ester Sahlin) as a source for reading the artist's despair and 'awakened misogyny' (26). Eva Arosenius presents her personal image of her late husband. She explains his aggression towards teachers, critics, etc. as irritation over being disturbed in his work, and describes his character as simultaneously naive, wise and ingenious. To her mind, there was no contradiction in his nature, and she states: 'He had nothing of the anxiety which is now constantly spoken of. He suffered from neither depressions nor fear of death. There was nothing neurotic in his character' (33). This appears to undermine the psychologizing interpretations of his art as a direct cartography over his personal emotions and development and the idea of the artist working in the shadow of death. That is, the person closest to Arosenius advocates leaving the notion of the aesthetically meaningful death, focusing instead on the aesthetically meaningful life.

Sven Sandström's monograph *Ivar Arosenius: His Art and Life* (1959) is an academic study, structured first in chronological chapters, followed by a number of thematic chapters. Much attention is thus directed towards Arosenius' life, but now not primarily to demonstrate his personal singularity but rather with a particular focus on his development as an artist. Thus, influences of many kinds are generously presented: emerging ideas and ideals about the painter and about art; artists, exhibitions Arosenius with likelihood or certainty visited, satirical journals Swedish and foreign, and not least literature that influenced him. Thus, the characteristics of Arosenius' art are contextualized and related to the cultural context in a new way: life to a great extent concerns intellectual and artistic development.

This approach to art history is paired with stylistic and thematic analyses of works, sometimes concerning influence more generally, sometimes through very distinct comparisons, sometimes concerning particularly Arosenian traits. While the widow of Arosenius the same year, in the print where Sandström also featured, stressed that he had neither depressions nor fear of death, Sandström invokes the aesthetically meaningful death. Arosenius was 'constantly pressed between two irreconcilable opposites: joy of living, and the sensation of the nearness of perishing' (46).

Arosenius' visit to Paris in 1904–5 expands, not without precedence, on Ester's ending their relationship, viewing his art as the sign of intense despair, rage and a new kind of misogyny: the paintings are described as 'excessive interjections which express his emotions with a sometimes inarticulate immediacy' (103–105; 222; the notion of hostility towards women is developed at

127–128). At the same time, Sandström posits, the paintings can be seen not only as the expressions of emotional conflict, but also as connecting to a genre related to Maeterlinck's symbolic dramas (198–199). In other words, technique, choice of motif and aesthetic influences are developed as well.

Sandström represents a new stage in interpreting Arosenius, providing more analysis, more genetic reasoning about artistic development, influences and relations between different versions of a work, and more relating to art-historical currents and contexts. In that process, life is an important means for explaining development, involving not least influences from schooling, friends, literature and art – but also with a distinct understanding of the artist's inner life as reflecting and reflected in the works.

A small volume was published by Kjell Hjern in 1961: *Arosenius and His City* (*Ivar Arosenius och hans stad*). The selection of images and the author did not really add anything to the discussion, but the double projections where Arosenius over-layered Gothenburg settings with oriental motifs were more clearly exemplified.

In 1963, Arosenius' friend Ernst Spolén devoted a whole book to his memories: *Ivar Arosenius: An Image of Recollection* (*Ivar Arosenius: En minnes-bild*). In this book, he expands considerably with a number of anecdotes from the periods they were together, presenting himself as a guardian who had to defend Arosenius after he had provoked different persons into fights. Arosenius' provocative nature is lavishly described, and a central place is given to the story of the physician's advice to Arosenius that alcohol was important for the ability to coagulate blood, which the young man took as an admonishment to extravagant consumption. Spolén suggests the image of St George and the dragon for Arosenius fighting his disease (1963, 54) and accentuates the question of blood by quoting a poem by Heine, pointing out that Arosenius would recite it from memory, stressing the final line: 'Und könnt' mein Herz verbluten unterdessen' (50–51). This connection between disease and paintings appears strong indeed, and Spolén sees Arosenius' relation to his own death as a key to his life (117–119). Here, Arosenius' memory is described as extraordinary, making him practically independent of models and motifs, collecting images all through the day, later to transform them into art. He is also quoted on his view of memory and art (31, cf. 89).

In a lavish catalogue to the exhibition at Nationalmuseum in 1978, entitled *Ivar Arosenius*, three scholars presented partially new images of Arosenius. Per Bjurström's biographical introduction summarizes points from Spolén's book – ordinated drinking, explorations of blood and bleeding – adding the importance of his daughter Lillan as an artistic symbol of life and living to the artist. In a subsequent chapter, Bjurström proposes three main components of Arosenius' art: the first is his need for artistic expression, the second is his ironic distance and the third is Arosenius' constant relating of art to his own life and situation (1978, 15). Bjurström explores the theme of blood not only through Spolén's connection between knight and dragon – Arosenius and disease – but also to explain more Paris images in terms of blood, bitterness and vindictiveness from love (26). Spolén's testimony of Arosenius' anxiety when awaiting the baby – would it be punished for the father's sins (Spolén 1963, 111)? – is developed into a conjecture about fear of transmitting his haemophilia (35–38); that is, connecting again disease and painting. Lillan's red dress is interpreted as a symbol of life, carrying the colour of healthy, oxygen-filled blood as opposed to the dark-coloured, lifeless blood connected to the dragon (57). Finally, Arosenius' self-portraits and tendency to place himself in his paintings are treated (57–66). In the background, one may sense the emerging interest of art history in self-portraits as artistic statements; that is, contributing a meta level. This approach can be found on occasion in later research, but Bjurström rather connects the paintings to Arosenius' personal life, dwelling on his identification with the character Noah and drinking.

Focusing on Arosenius' last years, 1905–8, Margaretha Rossholm develops a new kind of scholarly approach. Sketching the tradition of fairy-tale in Swedish and Scandinavian art of the late nineteenth century, Rossholm carefully illuminates the profound questioning and development of the genre Arosenius achieved, not only ironically challenging tradition, but also transforming it, transferring the fairy-tale motifs and themes from children's culture to something entirely new. Anti-heroism, distance and expressions of feebleness in general are central to this, and Rossholm clarifies not only by presenting the artistic tradition with precision, but also by demonstrating her points through technical analysis regarding perspective, imagery, motion, events, expressions and psychological states. Rossholm thus in a limited space achieves the first methodologically consistent treatment of Arosenius by focusing on his relation to tradition and influences, paired with a sensitive interpretation of artistic technique. On occasion she mentions the artist's life and ailment, but not in a way that actually concerns interpretation. Biographical aspects are as a rule restricted to genetic influences of an artistic kind.

In the last article in the catalogue, Nina Weibull dwells on the paintings with Arosenius' daughter as motif. She points to the fact that, unlike Carl Larsson, who would happily paint himself together with his children, Arosenius stays out of the pictures that feature his daughter – although he often leaves traces, such as his pipe or his paintings on the wall – suggesting that he considered her so special that he preferred not to portray her together with others (130–131). Weibull focuses on the group of motifs in which Lillan has a symbolic role as a tiny madonna or actualizing life, and demonstrates how Arosenius' and the viewer's perspective are made to follow that of the child.

During 1979 and 1980, an exhibition toured the cities of Düsseldorf, Ettlingen, Munich and Berlin. The catalogue, *Ivar Arosenius 1878–1909. Bilder und Graphik*, was quite extensive: some words by the Swedish ambassador Sven Backlund on the Swedish, yet supernatural character of Arosenius and a brief biographical introduction by Karl-Gustav Hedén were followed by commented images of sixty-eight works. The basis was the collection of the Gothenburg Museum of Art, and the comments were written by Björn Fredlund. The commented reproductions begin with four self-portraits which are tied to points in the artist's life, followed by a section, 'A love story', focusing on Ester Sahlin. Subsequent sections are 'Friends and foes' and 'Home and family', before turning to 'Social themes', 'Religion', 'Life and death', 'Eros', 'Inebriation' and 'Fairytale and myth'. For natural reasons, then, Arosenius' life and emotional state are often commented on. However, on several occasions, Fredlund formulates the comments tentatively and, after proposing an understanding of a painting against the artist's life, he proposes another artistic explanation by connecting to a number of pieces of influential art and literature. A catalogue based on the order of the paintings will necessarily follow the sections of the exhibition, which govern the understanding of the paintings. In this case life took a dominant position as an explanatory model, although supplemented with genetic arguments.

An exhibition catalogue, *Ivar Arosenius*, was printed in 1988. It contained a brief biography and three essays, the first of which was written by Nina Weibull and focused on Arosenius' relation to the feminine. According to Weibull, woman in Arosenius' art appears as the sex of life and strength, and she discerns three mythologies belonging to the three loves of his life, Ester, Gudrun and Eva. In this context, the 1904 paintings of women murder victims and some pictures of love for sale are explained as the result of an 'intensely expressed aggression towards woman as a sexual being' (24).

An essay by two medicine professionals, Kristina and Carl-Magnus Stolt, is devoted to haemophilia and its role in relation to Arosenius. While they take Arosenius' identification with St George against the dragon/disease as proposed by Spolén for granted, they reject Bjurström's interpretation of different nuances of blood in the artist's works, and understand the painting *Lustmurderer*, which Weibull took as a token of intense misogyny, as an expression of Arosenius' obsession with blood, suggesting the motif of blood as a therapeutic means for the artist. Describing the state of medicine at the time, they conclude that Arosenius must have known that his child would not develop haemophilia, but would be a genetic carrier to the next generation – i.e. again contradicting Bjurström (54–55). In a final essay, Gunnel Enby addresses the role of the daughter as Arosenius' motif and object of empathy.

An exhibition in Copenhagen in 1990 presented a catalogue, *Ivar Arosenius 1878–1909*, by Jens Bing, who stressed that Arosenius' greatest influence was satire. At the same time, his oil paintings prove that his closeness to satire could not have been caused by lacking skill. Bing points out that Arosenius' frequent use of watercolour was very ill suited for print and thus satiric journals. Prominently, Arosenius did not explore critical satire as much as a more multifaceted humour, not only chastising persons and social phenomena, but also admiring the beautiful in life. Tying this to Arosenius' ability to let the images tell the whole story without words, Bing presents a chronological survey of Arosenius' life and works, focusing on the techniques for presenting the paintings not as illusory renditions of the material world, but as a world in itself, created on its own conditions. The focus on artistic technique connects with biography not least through points such as polarity of life and death, light and shadow, and a present notion of death and awareness of what the artist would not be able to have.

In an article from 1995, Sven Sandström addressed the issue of Arosenius' very significant tendency to place himself in his paintings. While this trait was common also in artists like Albert Engström and Carl Larsson, Arosenius' own development of the approach was of a different kind. Focusing on one particular image, Sandström discusses the extent to which Arosenius' emotions and sense of guilt may be embedded in his art. In a small book from 1996 entitled *Ivar Arosenius* (*Första boken om Ivar Arosenius*), Per Bjurström gave a popular presentation of Arosenius both in Swedish and English. A presentation for the young, a *First Book on Ivar Arosenius*, was published by Lillemor Nordström the same year. In an exhibition in 2000, *Amateur/Enthusiast* (*Amateur/Eldsjäl*), Arosenius was presented as an example of the preceding turn of the century.

In the catalogue to an exhibition in 2005, *Ivar Arosenius: Akvareller/ Watercolours*, Joanna Persman concludes that the notion of the burlesque storyteller Arosenius has overshadowed questions of technique and medium. Persman thus examines his education not for biographical purposes, but in order to clarify distinctive artistic features and ideas, not least concerning the workings of memory. Through her focus on technique, Persman modifies the common notion of Arosenius as working swiftly and intuitively, showing that this capacity derived from careful and patient focus on a given set of motifs. Differences in his use of colour are also related chronologically, again without being related to the history of a soul. Persman focuses on Arosenius' self-portraits in a more art-focused way than has usually been done, examining a number of paintings as statements on art rather than on personality. The focus on formal aspects comes close to that of Rossholm, but concerning different aspects.

Björn Fredlund's *Ivar Arosenius*, printed in 2009, embraces a significant number of aspects of the artist – life as well as art. The structure is entirely chronological, comprising personal development but focusing very much on artistic development: the mastering of colour in Värmland, the child's perspective in Älvängen, etc. Fredlund details Arosenius' reading, once in a while underlining poems, books or authors that polarize emotional opposites: Heinrich Heine, Li Tai Po, Sigbjørn Obstfelder (54–55). Such influences concur with the image of Arosenius as the person and artist of opposites: on the one hand being his personal choice of reading, and on the other influencing the artist's mode of expression. In a similar way, Fredlund systematically maps influences from art, through books, education (on occasion) and visits to exhibitions and museums in Sweden and abroad. The influences are sometimes more general, sometimes very specific, clarifying individual works or periods. The break with Ester is also here seen as the cause of the Paris murder scenes, but the works are discussed not only biographically but as works of art in their own right (e.g. 107–108).

The Gothenburg coterie is described as 'a fairly late branch on an old, wide tree', and Fredlund aptly points out the precedent of the Norwegian 'Christiania Bohemianism' of the 1880s, where one maxim was: 'You shall write your life' (Du skal skrive dit liv). This commandment obviously suited Arosenius' art very well, incorporating to a great extent the artist and his friends in pictures and paintings.

Thus, Fredlund develops the biographical focus on Arosenius by connecting it to artistic development and formal aspects in a more coherent manner, still working in the chronological way but making it the development of an artist rather than of a soul. This approach had been prepared by works such as those of Rossholm and Persman, but is now applied to the life as a whole, which for natural reasons makes it impossible to develop the approach entirely consistently. A number of points thus open up for deliberation concerning what was personal expression of emotion (history of a soul) and what was deliberate artistic experiment and influences of an intellectual and artistic kind.

## 3.3 The Vangoghian Paradigm

Given the general scholarly development, it is hardly surprising that the studies on Arosenius have moved in the direction from the biographical towards the formal, from individual development (and aesthetic independence) towards artistic development and the general development of art. Nor is it, given the fact that several of the texts have been directed towards museum visitors and the public rather than towards the scholarly community, really surprising that the focus on Arosenius' inner life has been strong. The tendency to use the artist's paintings as sources for his inner life diminishes over the years, as does the focus on his early bohemian years. While biography remains interesting, it is more and more used not to reconstruct the history of a soul, but to clarify influences from reading and other art, in order to explain the artistic development and relate it to art history in general. The early cultic adoration is clearly connected to the will to extol the ingenuity of Arosenius and claim a position for him as cultural heritage, while later writings build cultural heritage on other arguments. These claims are substantiated by the blending of his life and his works in a way that goes directly back to Romantic notions of the isolated yet observing and digesting genius and Baudelaire's image of the artist. However, while the stress on the artist's freedom of impressions from other artists, polarization and contradictions are partly foregrounded in Romantic notions as well as the idea of the aesthetically meaningful death, the early focus on such traits and the early bohemian years appears to derive distinctly from a related, yet different, paradigm.

In essence, the development of Arosenius into cultural heritage is firmly based on a significant shift in the conception of an artist around the turn of the century, although not in a straightforward manner. It has been described by Nathalie Heinich as 'the Vangoghian paradigm', as the construction of van Gogh after his demise is more or less emblematic of it, although the development as such was of a general nature.

Obviously, the notions of genius and artistry through tradition have taken many guises, not least the connections between genius and insanity, thoroughly examined by Rudolf and Margot Wittkower. Madness and melancholy are traditional components which were also taken up by nineteenth-century psychoanalysis (Wittkower 1963, 288). Parts of the Vangoghian paradigm definitely were prepared (cf. e.g. Haynes 1997, 106–109), but the general ideal of an artist before it was very much a bourgeois notion of harmony and stability, modelled not least on the image of Johann Wolfgang von Goethe.

Although Romantic aesthetics had laid the foundation for the cult of genius and originality, the predominant paradigm of the nineteenth century was that aesthetic value was to be measured by established norms and conceptions of beauty. According to Heinich, at the time of his death in 1890, the thirty-seven-year-old van Gogh had received no recognition whatsoever, but from his death onwards a remarkable re-evaluation took place, first in reviews of exhibitions where his works featured, then gradually in exhibitions devoted only to him as well as studies, biographies and other publications which established a legend, or even hagiography of a new artist type:

> The new Vangoghian paradigm quite literally embodies a series of shifts in artistic value, from work to man, from normality to abnormality, from conformity to rarity, from success to incomprehension, and, finally, from (spatialized) present to (temporalized) posterity. These are, in sum, the principal characteristics of the order of singularity in which the art world is henceforth ensconced. That is the essence of the great artistic revolution of modernity, the paradigm shift embodied by van Gogh. (Heinich 1996, 146)

The Vangoghian paradigm had been evolving for two decades when Arosenius passed away, which means that, on the one hand, he was influenced by it himself, and on the other, the posthumous staging of Arosenius employed a fuller spectrum of aspects from it. Focusing for now on the reception of Arosenius, it is clear that many traits derive from the Vangoghian paradigm. The strong focus on personality and inner life is one; the recognition of deviation from norms rather than mastering of them, of rarity rather than conformity, is another. The idealization of the incomprehensible comes close, opening up for valuing the unusual, obscure or unexpected. The relation between present and posterity in Heinich's description is seminal: 'The attribution of guilt and the passage to posterity combine to transform the error committed by the artist's contemporaries, and especially art galleries, into a fault perpetrated against the artist, with the concomitant consequences, that is, debt, redemption, atonement. Hence, with the new paradigm, guilt bursts onto the artistic scene for the first time in history' (Heinich 1996, 147). Too late, excluding the chosen few, posterity recognizes the artist's greatness and thus its own guilt. The artist's suffering and gift to humankind parallels him with Christ, and his work is in a sense consecrated. This 'religious investment in aesthetics' and 'religious organization of the artistic world' Heinich connects to a general development where attending galleries and exhibitions engaged people as a partial substitution for going to church on Sundays, and reproductions of the works of art partially subsumed the commerce and use of religious objects in people's homes (Heinich 1996, 148–149).

The consecration of art is thus dependent on the technology of reproduction, which was discussed in Section 1 in connection with the development of the museum and changing notions of the 'original' at the turn of the century. In van Gogh's case, the development led to pilgrimage to places and veneration of objects in a way that is not applicable to the Arosenius case, and there are of course significant differences between the two as well as between their afterlives. Still, the Vangoghian paradigm can be seen as a forceful matrix for the staging of Arosenius, not only by posterity but also by himself. The first biography of van

Gogh established the strongly hagiographical structure of motifs: 'a calling; an uncommon man; isolation, marginality, unfitness for practical, social and commercial life; asceticism and poverty; disinterestedness; detachment from earthly goods and spiritual elevation; incomprehension and misappreciation by his contemporaries; martyrdom; finally, fulfilment in posterity' (Heinich 1996, 37). All of these traits, not least the quasi-religious adoration, were prominent already in the early works on Arosenius. The madness of van Gogh is not repeated in Arosenius, but, it seems, softened into a strong desire for non-conformity. Asceticism is not entirely congruent with Arosenius' 'high life', but is suggested as an involuntary effect of the lack of money, which Arosenius certainly suffered from, and which he for a long time chose rather than having to conform. His disinterestedness and detachment from earthly goods were most obvious in the descriptions of Arosenius' bohemerie – bohemerie being obviously the central feature of the Vangoghian paradigm and a seminal part of the Paris culture which Arosenius would enter. From early on, Arosenius was inspired by older bohemian spheres such as that of Albert Engström (Sandström 1959, 27–28). Martyrdom concerns the ailments and premature death, but in Arosenius' case his despairs in love may be considered an essential addition. Here, meaning is construed both through the aesthetically meaningful death and through the aesthetically meaningful suffering – emotional as well as physical. The displacement of religious structures onto the artist was most obvious in the early descriptions of the genius and cult, obviously interspersed with more traditional notions.

The notion of the aesthetically meaningful death, as proposed by Arping in the line from Bronfen, implies a male gaze on the female artist, and is founded on a female artist's life marked by attempts to find an alternative model for artistic identity, questioning traditionally male models by adding elements of fragility and powerlessness. While the aesthetically meaningful death is part of the Vangoghian paradigm, it appears that the female application of it is particularly pertinent to the reception of Arosenius. While forcefully employing the bohemian artist image, he questioned established models by destabilizing heroic ideals, presenting himself as decidedly anti-heroic and removed from masculine ideals and stressing male suffering in love and feebleness in his art: both staging himself within it and developing, for example, traditional fairy-tale motifs (see the discussion in subsection 4.1 of Arosenius' self-portraits). As we shall see, Arosenius would abandon the Vangoghian paradigm and model his persona into different forms. Posterity, however, appears to have been more reluctant to let go of the Vangoghian Arosenius.[10]

---

[10]  If a new biography of Arosenius were to be written, the point of departure might be that of Toril Moi's *Simone de Beauvoir: The Making of an Intellectual Woman* (1994), replacing a focus on

## 3.4 Vacillations in the Stagings of Arosenius

The Vangoghian paradigm appears to have been seminal for the early consolidation of Arosenius' position. To a great extent, Arosenius himself drew upon it in his early years, but while he very much abandoned it during his last years – his self-stagings are the subject of Section 4 – his death and the attempts to canonize him stirred up the Vangoghian notions to a much greater extent. Still, the Vangoghian paradigm cannot alone account for the strong focus on ambivalence, paradox and the shadow of death in the posthumous stagings of Arosenius: for these, biographism and the notion of the aesthetically meaningful death provide further explanations.

The images of Arosenius that have emerged contain a number of ambivalences concerning the meaning attributed to his works and the explanatory models for them. Contrary to the widespread notion of Arosenius' remarkable engagement with Lillan, his letters to his friends mention her only in a distanced manner (Fredlund 2009, 148–149). According to Spolén, immediately after her birth he left both mother and child – to inform his friends about the birth of his new-born daughter in person (Spolén 1963, 111). The question then is to what extent the works involving his daughter actually shed light on the inner life of Arosenius, and to what extent they shed light on the artist's choice of motifs and techniques, and his positioning of himself in the Swedish art market. It is clear that the home settings connect to the example of contemporary painters, at the same time as Arosenius twists the general trend into something artistically new. Given his increased efforts at a breakthrough in his last years, most ostensible perhaps in his choice of larger, more presumptuous canvases, the choice of motif could be seen as professional/strategic/technical rather than personal/emotional.

Arosenius' explorations of the home/family/child motifs obviously include the work he is best known for, the posthumously published *The Cat Journey* (*Kattresan*),[11] where his daughter, Lillan, is inscribed as the protagonist and at the same time addressee. This remarkable work seemingly attests to the father/artist's engagement with his daughter, but here, too, Arosenius develops

---

inner life and personality as an enigma with a focus on historically determined discursive constructions in Foucauldian fashion. That is, instead of cause–effect reasoning, psychologizing and attempting to clarify through environmental aspects, the 'polyphone' biography would follow certain narratives and themes, not least looking for contradictions and paradoxes (Possing 2015, 90–111; cf. Larsson 2007; Soussloff 1997, 24). It is difficult to divine how far such an interpretation would lead, but the Vangoghian paradigm is clearly a discursive complex that can illuminate a great deal of Arosenius' and posterity's stagings of the artist. For another perspective on the future of biographical research, see Guercio 2006, 283–293.

[11] See the app produced within the project by Jonathan Westin: itunes.apple.com/se/app/id1332811436?mt=8.

a technique for staging himself as an artist which had been prepared by other artists, most closely Carl Larsson, who had made a story with his son as the protagonist (Weibull 1978, 130–135). Even in this case, love and daughter form part of a business model – which of course does not say that there were no actual emotions. What appears certain is that Arosenius elaborately devised the self-staging.

From Carl Larsson, Bjurström proposes, Arosenius took over the cartoon format and his own child as protagonist, as well as the focus on riding and eating, at the same time as he refashioned the perspective and attitude in a congenial way. Bjurström draws attention to Arosenius' way of not telling the story about Lillan for others, but telling about Lillan for Lillan (Bjurström 1996, 46–50). This does not in itself mean that Arosenius was more private than Larsson. It does mean that he used the personal approach as a stylistic device in a product intended for the market, in a manner parallel to his way of exploring perspective in the paintings of Lillan, to which we will return in Section 4.

Another vacillation between personal emotions and artistic pragmatism concerns Spolén's editing of Arosenius' need for a bodyguard. In his book of 1963, Spolén described how he had assumed the function of bodyguard for Arosenius, who constantly provoked arguments and fights despite the extreme danger he ran if being hit and caused to bleed. The motivating emotion is evinced as a self-destructive challenge to his imminent death. As Fredlund has shown, in Spolén's manuscripts the provocations are presented as a deliberate way for Arosenius to provoke expressions and situations he could use as motifs, something that was edited out before printing. Fredlund comments that this calculating attitude does not seem to be congru-ent with the statements about Arosenius' choleric nature, and concludes that the contradiction may be only superficial: the provocations may have been emotional and analytic at the same time, giving the artist the opportunity to create art from experience (Fredlund 2009, 88–89). That is, as in the case of the daughter, Arosenius' seemingly overflooding emotionality can also be understood as pragmatic manoeuvring.

Yet one aspect of the constant diffusion between private and public Fredlund proposes: Arosenius was usually careful to also sign small things which were made in very private circumstances (Fredlund 2009, 89). And, of course, his constant use of himself and people around him in his paintings even further complicates the distinction between inner life and career.

What appears to be fairly certain is that Arosenius' perhaps most successful manoeuvre was his exploitation of the home/family/child motif. He had used his private sphere a great deal before as well, but here he appears to have found an amalgamation of life and art which appealed significantly to his time. This, of course, strongly called for psychologizing interpretations. The fusion of life and work, soul and art, in the reception of Arosenius is particularly clear in another important critic of the time, Karl Wåhlin, who in 1905 dismissed Arosenius for lacking an 'artistic sense of responsibility', but at the memorial exhibition of 1909 thought much more highly of Arosenius, saying that his person had been transformed (Gram 1996, 267–268). In effect, Wåhlin here formulates precisely the success of Arosenius' re-staging of himself into a traditional, solid, social artist: after starting out as a cynic and decadent, interesting for his violent temper, restless imagination and lyrical colouring,

> he becomes doubly enchanting as a fortunate turn in his fate refashions his inner being, and he is no longer just a witty head and an unusual artist, but his emotions become softened and refined, his view of life's fortunes and phenomena is supplemented with culture. He awoke from his bitterness and his curses as from a delirium, and his sensitive and fascinated heart was expanded with previously unknown lust and happiness.

The same set of ideas resounded in reception, not least influentially in the catalogue for the 1926 exhibition, where a brief introduction by Gunnar Wengström pointed out Arosenius' humour, connecting it with the doom of disease which drove him to 'challenge the reductive forces of nature, sound the depths and gloomy shadows of human life as well as try to catch the flickering illusion of happiness'. The fulfilment Wengström saw in Arosenius' urge for the consolidation of bourgeois life and family, which effected the rebirth: 'all that had been bitter and acrid became sunny, generous and flowering' as he learned to see through the child's eyes (Wengström 1926, vi–ix).[12]

In other words, only as Arosenius abandoned the Vangoghian paradigm did he win substantial recognition and make a breakthrough. General acclaim came as he established himself instead as the matured family man and artist.

However, while Arosenius forcefully directed his receivers towards his private person in a number of ways, this invitation appears to have led to a stronger psychologizing interpretation of him than warranted. Works of art have been interpreted as sources for his inner life to a degree that may not be entirely valid when it comes to interpretations of blood as a result of his ailment, when it may just as well be seen as a development of the broken/bleeding heart motif, or when murder scenes in line with cultural streams are interpreted as

---

[12] One of the more influential echoes of this idea is Knut Jaensson's 1944 reflections on an exhibition in *Konstrevy*, where he concludes that he prefers the 'master' to the 'bohemian', the 'ingenious ability for characterization, the exquisite use of colour and the brilliant saga fantasy' to the blasphemous focus on the Devil, Bacchus and the flesh of the youth (Jaensson 1944).

revenge or reaction to being left by his beloved. These motifs and their techniques will be further treated in Section 4.

To this, we may add that although Arosenius presented himself as an artist of opposites who liked to puncture high ideals, that may not legitimate the great number of descriptions of him as a person torn between the extremes on the whole. At least according to his wife, as we have seen, this image of him was largely exaggerated. To a considerable extent, these descriptions and interpretations appear to have been made as a result of the notion of the aesthetically meaningful death, which is by necessity a perspective laid from behind even if Arosenius knew that his life would not be very long. The notion of the aesthetically meaningful death invokes a paradigm which makes art a source to understand the artist's inner life, while his inner life is seen as expressed through the works. To Arosenius, the threat of death was aesthetically meaningful primarily insofar as it caused him to eventually hurry up his positioning and attempts to become an established artist. This he did by accentuating harmony and maturity rather than despair and polarization. That is, when imminent death actually dictated his work, his work changed in the direction of harmony and zest for life. Still, despair and polarization became the seminal part of posterity's notion of his meaningful death.

So, what can we conclude about Arosenius' inner life, personal development, artistic stagings and positioning? That they cannot really be distinguished from one another, but that reception has to a very high – although decreasing – degree made the artist's inner life key to his works, and at the same time made his works key to his inner life. The Vangoghian paradigm and the related notions of the aesthetically meaningful death appear to be the main conceptual embedding of the stagings of Arosenius both by himself and by his commentators. The artist abandoned them, but his audience did not.

Many of the features treated so far were obviously at hand also in Arosenius' actual life, and his self-fashioning was influenced by the contemporary notions and developments. While this section has been devoted to the narratives about Arosenius, the question remains: how did the artist stage himself? This is the topic of Section 4.

## 4 Staging the Self

Many of the notions about Arosenius that have dominated how his history was written were, obviously, prepared by himself. His frequent portrayals of himself and his friends, family and environments have invited a strongly biographical slant. Considering Arosenius' habit of signing even very private paintings, Fredlund concluded that he did not draw a distinct line between the public and the private. This, as we saw Fredlund propose, was consistent with the ideal of the bohemian lifestyle, as formulated by Hans Jæger, one of the authors of the Norwegian 'Christiania bohemians' of the 1880s. The first of his nine commandments was: 'You shall write your own life' (Du skal skrive dit eget liv; Fredlund 2009, 89, 51). The commandments were published in the journal *Impressionisten* 8, 1889, and although they are usually attributed to Jæger, he may have had no part in writing them, but rather have been the object of parody in them.[13] Those who were party to the writing of the commandments were in that case Oda and Christian Krohg, and if Jæger did actually write the commands, they were at least very closely associated. Arosenius would meet the Krohgs in Paris in 1904 and there would have been able to learn their views. Some of the commandments have a distinctly parodical ring, but Arosenius certainly in practice transposed the commandment from writing to painting and drawing: you shall paint your own life. The works of Arosenius thus to a remarkable extent are performative in the sense that they have been seminal in constructing an artist's role long after the artist's demise: staging him in the works themselves. However, his self-staging is complex and multi-faceted, and it differs from the stagings made after his death.

Besides a number of actual self-portraits, Arosenius is also known to have staged himself more vaguely in many works: placing himself in different contexts, or giving characters traits of his own face or person. The categories may not always be clearly discernible, but the following discussion will treat self-portraits proper; then 'self-pastings': traits of the self applied onto characters in artworks; then stagings of the self as one of the characters in other artworks; and finally, adding the point of perspective, self-stagings where the artist takes a position in regard to the motif; that is, inscribes himself outside of the motif, and shares this position with the viewer.

In this section, frequent reference will be made to images in the Arosenius Archive, but only the most important ones are included in this Element as such. The full range of illustrations can be found and downloaded at aroseniusarkivet.dh. gu.se/construing.pdf. Thus, illustrations enclosed in parentheses are in this Element, while illustrations that are only available for parallel viewing on a screen are in parentheses and brackets. The titles used are sometimes certainly Arosenius' own, but sometimes in all likelihood later creations. It is only when written on the painting that the title and year can be taken for granted with a fair amount of certainty.[14]

---

[13] The idea is suggested in the biographical novel *Jæger: En rekonstruksjon* by Ketil Bjørnstad (2001, 549–551).

[14] One kind of problematic dating is offered in *Portrait of Eva with Lillan in Locket* (Porträtt av Eva med Lillan i medaljong), which is dated 1905, but where the locket with Lillan, born in 1906, must have been added later (aroseniusarkivet.dh.gu.se/#/image/3923).

## 4.1 Self-Portraits

Generally, a portrait of the artist by him/herself calls for being understood as an artistic statement, and that is the case in a number of Arosenius' works. Equally generally, the private person must be involved in such paintings, and in Arosenius' case the personal tends to blend into the artistic statement in intricate ways, as much of his artistic status was congruent with how he appears to have wanted to be understood as a person.

Bjurström granted space for Arosenius' self-portraits and his tendency to place himself in his paintings (Bjurström 1978, 57–66). In the background, one may sense the emerging interest that art historians displayed in interpreting self-portraits as artistic statements; that is, as contributing a meta level. However, Bjurström rather connects the paintings to Arosenius' personal life, dwelling on his identification with the character of Noah and drinking. Arosenius' self-portraits were presented together in selections at the German exhibition in 1979, where four self-portraits were connected to points in Arosenius' biography but also to aesthetic influence, and the Gothenburg exhibition of 2009–10, both curated by Fredlund. In his monograph, Fredlund devotes attention to particular self-portraits, clarifying not least symbolic traits (Fredlund 2009, 73–74, 143–145, 166). Before that, Persman had examined a number of paintings as statements on art rather than on personality.

Self-portraits proper, where the artist is his only model, range from not very statement-like images to paintings laden with statements. The most distinctly statement-like self-portraits are from 1905, 1906 and 1908.

The 1905 *Self-Portrait with Allegorical Background* (Självporträtt med allegorisk fond, Figure 1) involves the beholder in a suggestively elusive manner. With a dark forest in the background, a church or possibly a castle emerges with a naked, pregnant Venus followed by the Grim Reaper and a jester. In front of a watery surface, the artist looks intently towards the beholder. He does not appear powerful, but rather playfully questioning the foundations of our borders between real life and fantasy – this questioning of boundaries seems to be underscored by the artist's somewhat androgynous traits. As Persman emphasizes, the composition places the artist firmly in the background setting: the borders between dream and reality are erased, and the artist is placed in a medium position between the viewer and the world of the fairy-tale – nature, Venus, death and joke being among the main characteristics of Arosenius' paintings (Persman 2005, 9). The question is: is the artist actually looking at the beholder? His expressive eyes actually appear to fix on something to the left of the beholder: does he see something behind our back? A scenery corresponding to that which he has painted behind himself? In that case, we may have to

**Figure 1** *Self-Portrait with Allegorical Background* (Självporträtt med allegorisk fond, 1905)

conclude that the artist's motifs are what is to be found in everyone's life, or at least they can be found by us all if we look for them.

*Self-Portrait with Garland* (Självporträtt med blomsterkrans, 1906, Figure 2) presents an Arosenius with both a sweater and a garland that he actually owned, as testified by photographs (the garland still exists). In 1928, Asplund described it as

> not entirely lifelike, but an interpretation of his nature, the Dreamer, who around his forehead feels the scent of the flowers of fantasy. ... Did he not feel the mild, beautiful powers in life, the flowering and smelling, the living and creating, coming closer to him, wishing to erase that bitterness and cynicism that had taken root in his heart? The flowers are more than an affected poetic arrangement, they are a confession. ... fantasy and reality do not resemble each other, and fantasy was more true to him. (Asplund 1928, 102)

In stark contrast to this psychologizing description, Persman in 2005 demonstrated how the self-portrait presents several layers of meaning, first as the flower as a traditional symbol of art was frequently used in portraits and self-

**Figure 2** *Self-Portrait with Garland* (Självporträtt med blomsterkrans, 1906)

portraits of artists around the turn of the century, then by connecting the garland to the crown of thorns and thus to suffering, and to the laurel wreath as a sign of eternity and immortality – an unintentional prophecy of the artist's reception after his death (Persman 2005, 21). Fredlund in 2009 added analysis of the background, both the flower supported by a trellis probably referring to the recently overcome medical crisis and the dragonflies symbolizing, on the one hand, life's brevity but, on the other, as they are mating, the continuance of life (Fredlund 2009, 143–145).[15] This contribution does add a biographical perspective, but one which can also be understood as artistic statements, as

---

[15] Mankell 2003 in a general study of self-portraits points out that the flower may be connected to Madame Blavatski's 'symbolist flower' and that the wreath has a tradition of signifying artistship (156–167).

Arosenius definitely defined the oppositions of fragility–strength and life–death in his artistic programme.

Arosenius' self-portraits during the late Älvängen period are few, but one from 1908 (Figure 3) also is of a particularly representative character, being intended for the Salon d'automne in Paris (Fredlund 2009, 168). Far away is the bohemian character of his youth: here emerges a stable and focused person. The background is the landscape of his family home Älvängen, but turned into an Arcadia, with a temple, naked women dancing, a bird of paradise and other motifs he cherished – an inebriated man and an oriental embracing a woman. The stars, Fredlund suggests, may be understood as symbols of the freedom of fantasy (Fredlund 2009, 166–168). The motifs are not allegorical in the same way as in the 1905 self-portrait, but they, too, distinctly represent Arosenius' art. That is, while the 1905 self-portrait focused on artistic statement, the 1908 one retains that focus but at the same time adds other layers by enveloping the artist

**Figure 3** *Self-Portrait* (Självporträtt, 1908)

in his actual life's settings. This merging of life and work is readily taken as yet another artistic statement: the artist had always merged life and art, but nowhere more than in Älvängen, where his home became the dominant scenery (to which we shall soon return). It thus connects to contemporary self-portraits in home settings by other artists, but uses the landscape to project the creations of the artist's fantasy. Another side of this painting's adherence to a more representative kind of self-portrait is that the role of family father results in a considerably more masculine representation of the artist. Usually, he had portrayed himself with bad carriage, suggesting both limited power and will to conform, and as another kind of deviation from norms, he could present himself with more or less androgynous traits. So, the *Self-Portrait with Allegorical Background* from 1905 presents the artist as following neither gender ideals nor social ones, instead destabilizing the boundaries between real life and imagination, while *Self-Portrait with Garland* from 1906 presents the artist as feebly translucent. The Älvängen self-portrait from 1908, on the other hand, is distinctly about power, might, decisiveness and male responsibility – underscored by his beard and the cigar in his hand, all very much in line with the artistic ideal of maturity and consolidation which we saw expressed by Wåhlin in 1909 and Wengström in 1926, distinctly deviating from the Vangoghian paradigm.[16]

These three self-portraits, the most obviously statement-like in Arosenius' oeuvre, illustrate his progression towards an entirely different role than the one in which he had worked during his youth. Symptomatically, the young bohemian Arosenius seems not to have indulged in these kinds of more or less official proclamations. However, an eloquent demonstration of the role he now gradually abandoned is the blasphemous vagabond in *Self-Portrait in the Gallery of the Tabernacle* (Självporträtt på läktaren i tabernaklet, 1903, Figure 4).

If the titles attributed to them are by Arosenius himself, two self-portraits from 1903 display an interesting transfer from inner life to artistry. In *Sunset* (Solnedgång, Figure 5) the artist, like a Pied Piper of Hamelin, conjures up snakes and devils. While the motif eloquently speaks of the power of the artist and of art, and the evil creatures seem motivated by the fact of night approaching, it does not appear as self-evident that the artist plays in order to free humankind of them, as the Pied Piper did. Rather, he appears to be conjuring them up to the world. However, it does not seem at all certain that he can control them. Another, contemporary, version of the same motif is entitled *Anguish*

---

[16] Cf. Mankell 2003, where the cigar is rather seen as a sign of self-indulgence and simultaneously self-destruction (118–119). The way the artist holds the cigar is also reminiscent of a camera trigger, suggesting the medium of photography rather than painting and thus accentuating the contrast between real world and imagination in the scene (brought to my attention by Christine Sjöberg).

**Figure 4** *Self-Portrait in the Gallery of the Tabernacle* (Självporträtt på läktaren i tabernaklet, 1903)

(Ångest, Figure 6). This one adds skeletons to the devils and snakes and presents the artist's face, suggesting terror and threat which are lacking in the other painting. The title further directs attention to the artist's own inner life insofar as it appears that his playing the flute here is to be taken as an attempt at defending himself and fending off the creatures of anxiety, appearing to be his inner demons. By contrast, in the *Sunset* version of the motif, the focus appears to be on his artistic power. That is, one of the variations of the motif presents the demons as a personal fear, while the other presents them as the artist's creations and suggests artistic control.

**Seclusion:**    A number of self-portraits present Arosenius as a person rather than an artist, although genius – or will to genius – can sometimes be extrapolated either through critical attitude ([Figure 7]) and/or intently scrutinizing eyes. A self-portrait from 1902 ([Figure 8]) has been shown to employ the same intense gaze that his friends and colleagues Ole Kruse and Gerhard Henning

**Figure 5** *Sunset* (Solnedgång, 1903)

also experimented with (Fredlund 2009, 61–64). In the case of *Self-Portrait with Hen and Pigs* (Självporträtt med höns och grisar, 1903?, Figure 9), the artist is clearly depicted as an imaginary genius, but one who is also secluded from the world's delights (*Ivar Arosenius 1878–1909. Bilder und Graphik*, 20–22; *Ivar Arosenius 1878–1909*, 32–34). More peculiarly, as the surroundings are interspersed with outlines of imaginary characters, this painting suggests that the artist is actually secluded even from his own imaginations. A presumably earlier version of the motif ([Figure 10]) makes a more personal impression, with no clear proposition about imagination or artistry, but simply introvert solitude. As in the case of *Anguish* and *Sunset*, it seems that the artist's less developed version is more personal and has less meta-statement. Another way of presenting the distance between the artist and the world is presented in *Self-Portrait on Cloud* (Självporträtt på moln, 1907 [Figure 11]), where the

**Figure 6** *Anguish* (Ångest, 1903)

artist has written: 'Self-biography: Hell, I am so talented!' (Själfbiografi: Fan, hvad jag är begåfvad!). He is known to have exclaimed this remark on repeated occasions, and his own illustration of it presents him floating on a cloud above the roof-tops.

**Viewer:** A few self-portraits convey the artist as a viewer: in *The Book of Life* (Livets bok, 1908, Figure 12), Arosenius presents himself as twin characters reading a book, understandable as the world, in two very different ways. The light and smiling Arosenius enjoys; the dark and critical Arosenius is full of doubt. In *Self-Portrait by Easel* (Självporträtt vid staffli, 1901, Figure 13), it may be that Arosenius models himself on Carl Larsson's self-portrait *In Front of the Mirror* (Framför spegeln, 1900[17]): in this case, the artist is scrutinizing

---

[17] commons.wikimedia.org/wiki/File:Framför_spegeln.jpg.

**Figure 9** *Self-Portrait with Hen and Pigs* (Självporträtt med höns och grisar, 1903?)

himself painting (Persman 2005, 20). However, the resemblance to Larsson's painting is not very significant, and as Persman points out, Arosenius was left-handed, which means he is not seen through a mirror as Larsson was. There is thus no urgent cause to posit a mirror, and if there is no mirror, the represented artist is actually viewing not himself but the viewer – and simultaneously painting the viewer. As we shall see, Arosenius would develop other ways of picturing himself as viewer in his self-stagings.

**Medial double-layering:** In a self-portrait from Paris, Arosenius pictures himself in a way that appears entirely focused on his personal emotions and state of mind, yet creates the painting so as to draw attention to its status of artefact and mixture of reality layers. *Those Beautiful Days Are Passed* (Il sont passé ces

**Figure 12** *The Book of Life* (Livets bok, 1908)

**Figure 13** *Self-Portrait by Easel* (Självporträtt vid staffli, 1901)

beaux jours [IA's spelling], 1903, Figure 14)[18] presents Arosenius doubly: in the foreground, tears falling from his eyes, he speaks the French words that give the painting its name. In the background, on a desolate square inhabited only by a public urinal and two *gendarmes* looking suspiciously at him, another Arosenius walks hunched up and cursing – the title is in French but the curses in Swedish. While the spatial background may be taken as a temporal background to the foregrounded Arosenius who appears to be addressing someone French, on both grounds comic strip or cartoon technique is used to create distancing effects beside that of doubling the character: first, by making the same person speak in two languages; second, by introducing a comic strip balloon containing the French words, but one that stretches out like a road towards the urinal, repeating the message; third, by introducing a second comic strip technique for the curses in Swedish, simply spreading them over the square to the effect that they seem to form a paving and thus blending the level of expression with the level of image;

**Figure 14** *Those Beautiful Days Are Passed*
(Il sont passé ces beaux jours [IA's spelling], 1903)

---

[18] Possibly inspired by the French translation of a song by Goethe, the beautiful days being the days of love.

and fourth, by employing the techniques of the comic strip for a scenery which contains nothing comic – only pain and desperation.

The three self-portraits treated initially are the ones which most distinctly aim at presenting the artist to the public and establishing him in a specific role. Their development over time is substantial: from the 1905 elusive and mocking artist who suggests that his world of fantasy is to be found also behind the beholder, paralleling the elusiveness of worlds with elusiveness of gender, over the feeble and translucid artist of 1906 to the powerful and manly artist of 1908. These three statements are paralleled by the less 'official' self-portraits which often supply meta-perspectives or question the artist's medium in other ways. To these could be added a number of other self-portraits of varying degree of elaboration, mostly from the early years, which strengthen the impression of the artist's deliberate move from bohemian rebel and outsider towards the matured painter and family father in combination: a move from the Vangoghian paradigm to the more traditional paradigm of success ([Figures 15–25]).

## 4.2 Blood

A number of self-portraits and probable self-stagings do not seem to function as artistic statements at all, but have rather been understood biographically, as personal expressions. To a great extent they revolve around the issue of blood. In a letter in 1902 (Figure 26), Arosenius painted himself suffering from his disease, at that time manifesting itself in problems with his joints, here the knee (a side effect of the haemophilia). While he did not draw distinct lines between the private and the public, there are no other direct representations of his ailment. However, his use of blood has often been seen as an expression of his fear or handling of the disease. One aspect that speaks against that view is that in his self-portraits, the use of blood appears to develop from the image of the broken heart as a very deliberate development of traditional literary meta-phors, gaining momentum through the incompatibility between the medium of words and the medium of image. One version of heart and love, painted in 1903 (Figure 27), presents him despising worldly temptations as his over-dimensioned heart is filled with Ester Sahlin. The image so exaggerates and explores stereotypical metaphors of heart and love: the heart being filled with the beloved, the image of the beloved residing in the heart. (The blue ribbon, barely visible behind the heart, is explicated with the words 'Note! Blue ribbon' (OBS! Blå bandet), the symbol and name of a temperance society, suggesting that he scorns not only women but also alcohol.) The image certainly is personal, but the bleeding clearly connects to literary stereotypes and does not seem to be invoked by attention to the disease.

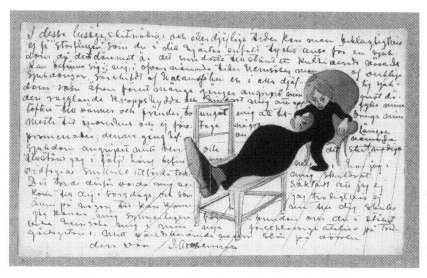

**Figure 26** Letter to Signe Lagerlöw-Sandell, 1902

**Figure 27** *Self-Portrait with Image of Ester Sahlin* (Självporträtt med Ester Sahlins bild, 1903)

In the same line, other variations on the heart–love theme instead explore and exaggerate the concretion of the literary metaphor of the broken heart: in a painting for some reason known as *The Broken Heart* (Det brustna hjärtat, 1901, Figure 28), a winged female character has stolen the heart of a character with Arosenius' traits rather than broken it, and the natural(istic) effect of the heart being removed is severe bleeding. The angel-like winged female thus, it appears, paves the way for the approaching demons of anxiety. The metaphorical dimension is retained by bewilderment and imminent haunting. The metaphor 'stolen heart' is the obvious focus; to the extent the metaphor of the 'broken heart' is relevant, it too would generate bleeding. In *Self-Portrait with Arrow in Bleeding Heart* (Självporträtt med pil i blödande hjärta, 1902, Figure 29), the metaphorical layer of Cupid's arrow is developed into its fleshly results, again profuse bleeding. The theme of the bleeding heart is also varied in *Self-Portrait* (Själfporträtt, 1903 [Figure 30]). A further variation of the love–heart metaphor into overly concrete imagery is *Self-Portrait with Heart in Hand* (Självporträtt med hjärta i handen, 1903–4; this appears to be the first time Arosenius uses heart

**Figure 28** *The Broken Heart* (Det brustna hjärtat, 1901)

**Figure 29** *Self-Portrait with Arrow in Bleeding Heart* (Självporträtt med pil i blödande hjärta, 1902)

**Figure 31** *Self-Portrait with Heart in Hand* (Självporträtt med hjärta i handen, 1903–4)

and blood as symbols (Fredlund 2009, 74), Figure 31). 'Heart in hand', corresponding to 'heart on one's sleeve', invokes the candid, unguarded showing and following of emotions, while the painting visualizes the effects. The hat in his other hand enforces the theme by proposing him as a beggar in emotions.

These images clearly attest to ingenious variation and questioning of traditional motifs and concepts – a kind of variation Arosenius performed in many fields, but it is less clear how any of them might derive from Arosenius' being a bleeder.

The issue of blood warrants a deviation from paintings which do not portray the artist but are usually considered to express him in other ways. In 1909, Romdahl claimed that as Arosenius lived more in the world of the fairy-tale than in the world of the real, the heroes in his fairy-tale works of necessity always or mostly carry his traits (Romdahl 1909, 6). In this vein, Asplund in 1928 interpreted a painting of *St George Fighting the Dragon* (Sankt Göran och draken, 1903, Figure 32) as autobiographical: the princess defended being Ester Sahlin and the dragon's blood gushing out relating to Arosenius' constant attention to his disease (Asplund 1928, 63–65). Asplund's psychologizing interpretations were confirmed by Spolén, who attested that Arosenius would symbolize his relation to his disease by St George fighting the dragon (Spolén 1956, 54) and followed up not least by Bjurström, who developed a broad blood symbolism (Bjurström 1978, 16). Spolén, as mentioned, reported that Arosenius once recited a poem of Heine, stressing the final words about his bleeding heart: the poem as such falls directly under the matrix of wounded hearts as treated earlier.[19] After the testimony of Spolén the biographical slant can hardly be denied, but it is a curious fact that the knight bears no obvious resemblance to Arosenius. As pointed out by Rossholm, Arosenius' fairy-tale

---

[19] Spolén 1963, 51. The sonnet, from Heine's *Buch der Lieder*, reads:

> Hüt dich, mein Freund, vor grimmen Teufelsfratzen,
> Doch schlimmer sind die sanften Engelsfrätzchen.
> Ein solches bot mir einst ein süßes Schmätzchen,
> Doch wie ich kam, da fühlt ich scharfe Tatzen.
> Hüt dich, mein Freund, vor schwarzen, alten Katzen,
> Doch schlimmer sind die weißen, jungen Kätzchen.
> Ein solches macht ich einst zu meinem Schätzchen,
> Doch tät mein Schätzchen mir das Herz zerkratzen.
> O süßes Frätzchen, wundersüßes Mädchen!
> Wie konnte mich dein klares Äuglein täuschen?
> Wie konnt dein Pfötchen mir das Herz zerfleischen?
> O meines Kätzchens wunderzartes Pfötchen!
> Könnt ich dich an die glühnden Lippen pressen,
> Und könnt mein Herz verbluten unterdessen!

**Figure 32** *St George Fighting the Dragon* (Sankt Göran och draken, 1903)

heroes are programmatically, as a reaction to the genre, characterized by a lack of heroism, and instead feebleness (Rossholm 1978, 72). In this case, the red dress of the princess does recall Ester Sahlin who was regularly painted in red, but the knight does not have the clear traits of the artist pasted onto him and he shows nothing of feebleness. What is evident is that Arosenius here twists the dragon motif, focusing on the blood from its wounds, in a way reminiscent of other twists of dragons, most remarkably in the motherly loving dragon and her innocently lethal offspring in *Evil Powers* (Onda makter, 1907, Figure 33 [and 34]), but more similar, probably, to *The Dragon* (Draken, 1906, Figure 35), *St George and the Dragon* (St Göran och draken, 1906 [Figure 36]) and *The Dragon Fight* (Drakstriden, 1907 [Figure 37]).

We have seen that several self-portraits explore the motif of blood, often in less profuse ways, but constantly challenging and questioning traditional metaphors connecting love with blood and heart. While they have often been associated with the artist's disease, grouped together, they appear as very deliberate variations on traditional blood imagery, a play with literary stereotypes.

**Figure 33** *Evil Powers* (Onda makter, 1907)

**Figure 35** *The Dragon* (Draken, 1906)

Another issue of blood in relation to biography has concerned Arosenius' Paris period, where Sandström and others interpreted bloody murder scenes as results of misogyny and excessive emotions caused by the break-up with Ester Sahlin (Sandström 1959, 103–105, 127–128, 222). Arosenius certainly did produce a number of strong and sometimes gory paintings in Paris. The most conspicuously bloody ones portray men slaughtering women: *A Parisian Murder Drama* (Ett parisiskt morddrama (Figure 38)), *Lustmurderer* (Lustmördare, Figure 39)) and not only a woman in *Wedding Murder* (Bröllopsmord [Figure 40]), all 1904. Other paintings, too, have been connected to the Paris state of emotions, such as *Those Beautiful Days Are Passed* (Figure 14) and *When the Flower Burst* (När blomman sprack ut [Figure 41]),

**Figure 38** *A Parisian Murder Drama* (Ett parisiskt morddrama, 1904)

**Figure 39** *Lustmurderer* (Lustmördare, 1904)

where the colour of the flower has been connected to Ester Sahlin's dress (Montgomery 1986, 129, cf. Fredlund 2009, 109). Stolt and Stolt (1988) rejected misogyny in the murder scenes, explaining them instead as fixation with blood.

However, these paintings could be understood as genre paintings just like the other ones Arosenius produced, which do not invite speculations about misogyny or fixation with blood. Asplund, Romdahl and Fredlund have pointed to the fact that the murder motif connects to the horror novels which were popular at the time. Fredlund explains that Arosenius changed the name of *A Parisian Murder Drama* into *A Parisian Feuilleton* (En parisisk följetong) when presenting it at an exhibition in Stockholm in 1905 (Fredlund 2009, 108; cf. Asplund 1928, 140; Romdahl 1909, 12). By changing its title, Arosenius appears to deliberately point us at the narrative genre rather than at his inner life. Furthermore, sex murder had received lavish attention through the focus on Jack the Ripper in 1888, and was a developing theme in literature, art and movies (Hermansson 2020). It has been pointed out that it was in Paris that Arosenius started exploring the motifs and techniques of the saga (Sandström 1959, 124), and the arguments for connecting the murder motifs to his inner state at the time may not be stronger than they would be for connecting the saga motifs to his inner state at the time. The question then is whether Arosenius' paintings need explaining both from his life and passions, and from aesthetic influence.

While the association of blood and haemophilia is close at hand not only for posterity but also must have been so for Arosenius himself, it remains unclear to what extent his biography and a posited anxiety may be attributed explanatory value. Contextualized according to literary and artistic traditions and movements, as well as to artistic techniques and motifs, the works of art seem to propose other explanations and connect to other contexts. On the one hand, Arosenius used the blood and heart motif to exaggerate and toy around with traditional literary stereotypes; on the other hand, he developed the popular theme of lustmurder.

## 4.3 Self-Pastings

A number of paintings cannot be described as placing the artist himself within the scenery, but rather as lending characters traits of the artist. The borders are not entirely clear, but self-pastings suggest the artist's own person in a more indirect manner than the self-portraits, often in a kind of fairy-tale scenery. *The Broken Heart* (Figure 28) mentioned earlier is one example of self-pasting rather than self-portrait: a few other examples will be described here in order to clarify this particular kind of self-staging.

In *Lagging Behind* (Eftersläpet, 1902 [Figure 42]), a faun with Arosenius' face is involved in a contradictory scene of love with a nymph. An entirely different example, which poses the question whether it should be understood as a genuine expression of Arosenius' inner life or an exploitation of his own emotions, is *Antichrist* (Antikrist, 1906 [Figure 43]). A man with Arosenius' traits looks down at his new-born child, which has distinctive features of a devil, while the mother lies in the bed with a sign of death over her. This was composed just before the birth of his child and is readily understood as a projection of his personal anxieties (Sandström 1995; this picture was also developed into a series [Figure 44]), although there is nothing to suggest that fear of the mother dying would have been a particular concern.[20]

In one of Arosenius' fairy-tale series, *The Tale of the Magician and the Wonderful Bird* (Sagan om trollkarlen och den underbara fågeln, 1908 [Figure 45]), the magician lovingly chases the woman bird over land, sky and sea, but in vain. In the final picture he has fallen to the ground and

---

[20] Cf. aroseniusarkivet.dh.gu.se/#/image/4487 and aroseniusarkivet.dh.gu.se/#/image/4078.

another bird is picking his heart out, with yet more birds ominously approaching. There is no explanation for the magician's being a magician in this story of hopeless love, but as it is distinctly about pursuing dreams and imagined states, at the cost of life, the identification between magician and artist is not very remote – especially as the magician in the final picture, but not before, is endowed with Arosenius' traits (Fredlund 2009, 186; on the of notion artist–magician, see e.g. Roberts 1990, 182–186). (There is a sketch self-portrait ([Figure 46]), not mentioned earlier, where Arosenius seems to draw a similar turban on himself – but it could also simply be his hair (cf. [Figure 19]).[21] The series *Ben Oni's Dream* (Ben Oni's dröm, 1908) is similar in setting and story, but the main character is not attributed Arosenian traits.)

In a series from 1908, *Spirited Away* (Den bergtagne [Figure 47]), a character with Arosenius' traits plus a long beard meets a naked female, is lured into the mountain and in the following image returns, much aged and enfeebled (while the horse remains in the same day and the tree it is tied to has lost its leaves; see Rossholm 1978, 105). The motif of being enticed or abducted into a mountain by trolls or other creatures is common in folk-tales, but mostly involves women or children. When Arosenius makes the motif centre around a man, he actualizes both Tannhäuser and the tradition of the Isle of Bliss, where the central character is a man, and seduction rather than abduction is the main concern. Attraction and lust are thus the main reasons for the departure from the real world into the realm of imagination, and the motif is strongly connected to literary explorations of the role of art and the artist, not least in Scandinavia (see Hermansson 2010). In the most prominent Swedish example, P. D. A. Atterbom's *The Isle of Bliss* (Lycksalighetens ö, 1824), the hero returns from the Isle of Bliss only to discover that time has stood still there: he is the same age as when he left, but the world has changed and aged. Atterbom's model was French and the notion was also expressed, for example, in Novalis' magical idealism and idea of the true seeker (cf. Roberts 1990, 184). Arosenius makes the opposite: the man who leaves for the world of magic and, we may take it, imagination comes back aged and worn. His obvious resemblance to the artist himself presents us with a distanced and hesitant stance towards the attractions of the flesh, imagination and art, the artist himself paying a costly tribute.

The self-pastings, like the self-portraits, are sometimes used to describe the conditions of art and artist, but they do not constitute artistic statements in the way self-portraits can do.

---

[21] Pointed out to me by Björn Fredlund. Cf. Sandström 1959, 59.

## 4.4 Self-Staging: The Artist Viewed

Besides the self-portraits proper, focusing only on himself, and the self-pastings, where more or less clearly discernible traits of the artist are found in characters not necessarily identified with the artist, Arosenius staged himself in a number of artworks together with different characters and to different effects. These self-stagings can be divided into three categories: those presenting the artist viewed, those presenting the artist viewing and those simultaneously presenting the artist viewing and negatively, potentially viewed, where he so to speak has left his place in the scenery and taken a position behind, or rather in front of, the scene. There are a number of characters with which Arosenius has been taken to have identified, but the following discussion will be limited to instances where Arosenius in one way or other painted himself into the work of art.

Arosenius constantly painted his surroundings, friends and other persons around him, and placed himself in these sceneries as well – sometimes as ambitious works, sometimes as sketches or letters. It was part of his heritage from the satirical journal to include himself: anti-bourgeoisie as well as immodest self-portraiture had been thoroughly developed by Albert Engström and the magazine *Strix* (Sandström 1995, 43–46 [Figures 48–52]).

Works presenting Arosenius and his colleagues/friends as bohemians obviously function both biographically and on a meta level, conveying understandings of the artist Arosenius. The meta level is underscored significantly in paintings where Arosenius stages himself among actual persons but in fantastic settings, or in entirely created contexts. *Life and Its Baggage* (Livet och dess tross, 1906, Figure 53) pictures a wedding procession with him, his wife, relatives and others in a way that underscores his opposition to common norms, the bride being obviously pregnant and dressed in red, and their carriage deviating from the common road to the dismay of the followers. The power of imagination over life is directed to the question of being an artist by the Pegasus pulling the carriage not only away from the road, but also away from the ground.

*The Mill of Bliss* (Lycksalighetens kvarn, 1905, Figure 54) places Arosenius centrally as the transformer of life, driving a mill which converts the stiff, dirty and rigid everyday into the colourful, light and happy world of fancy. The mill's implication of art is underscored both by the figure of Arosenius himself and by a Pegasus: in this painting, the affirmation of imagination and art seems to be unreserved.[22] The Pegasus is also used in variations on *The Tavern* (Värdshuset,

---

[22] The motif appears to be inspired by the 'Dalmålning' tradition expressed in Hjelt Per Persson's 1843 *The Mill of Old Hags* (Kärringkvarnen, also known as *The Mill of Youth* (Ungdomskvarnen); digitaltmuseum.se/011013836043/karringkvarnen-dalmalning-av-hjelt-per-persson-1843-nm-inv-nr-12382). See Svärdström 1944, 121 and Jansson 2014, 66–67. The

**Figure 53** *Life and Its Baggage* (Livet och dess tross, 1906)

**Figure 54** *The Mill of Bliss* (Lycksalighetens kvarn, 1905)

1904 [Figures 55, 56]), where the focus is not on the artist's production but rather on his temptations. A general air of fatigue modulates the motif.

In *Apotheosis* (Apoteos, 1906, Figure 57) Arosenius more distinctly, yet paradoxically, pinpoints his own position as an artist. The painting conveys

---

direct inspiration, however, appears to be a separate print as described in Sandström 1959, 133, who also mentions one more painting by Arosenius on the motif.

**Figure 57** *Apotheosis* (Apoteos, 1906)

a liberated, or libertine, *joie de vivre* in a tavern setting, but by the means of a very realistic detail which he had developed in naturalistic studies such as portraits. This inebriated festivity is accompanied by Arosenius himself in a peculiarly double position. In the composition he is not very visible, placed in a remote corner. In the action, however, he is central, as he plays the violin and thus in a sense orchestrates everything, in a way parallel to the painter's composing his work. Arosenius' staging himself as the artist conducting the tribute to life and lust is paradoxical in the way he shifts medium from painting to music: he is known not to have been very gifted musically (Sandström 1959, 171). The pretensions of the title are relativized significantly by the realistic and temporal setting, presenting the artist's accomplishment as powerful, but creating only a momentary illusion of apotheosis and liberation from the everyday. The illusory state is emphasized by a centrally positioned, already disillusioned man, ridding the painting of every metaphysical aspect and turning the title into irony.

## 4.5 Self-Staging: The Artist Viewing

The standard mode of self-portraits is that the artist looks at the beholder (and thus at him/herself). While this creates a sense of presence, there is no object of the artist's gaze in the painting itself. In some cases, however, Arosenius explores less conventional modes of viewing, by also elaborating on the object of the gaze. As we have seen, in *The Book of Life* he presented himself as reader/interpreter rather than conveyer. In *Apotheosis*, the artist as directing the crowd to an extent has the character of a viewer of the spectacle. In *Self-Portrait by Easel*, the artist looks right at the viewer in a way that turns the viewer into the object of the painting that is being composed, and in *Self-Portrait with Allegorical Background*, the artist appears to be watching something behind the viewer. In other works, the artist stages himself as a viewer in considerably more elaborate ways.

In *Toilette* (1905, Figure 58) Arosenius portrays his wife-to-be dressing, framing himself as the motif of a painting on the wall, happily and humorously gazing at her (Sandström 1959, 43–44; a more conventional version where the artist paints himself adoring his wife is *Quiet* (Tyst, 1905 [Figure 59]). A painting where the artist's traits are not visible, but the title suggests his presence as viewer, is *If I Were King* (Si j'étais roi, 1907? [Figure 60]). Here, simply the fascination of a particular motif is suggested.

In *Paris Wedding* (Bröllop, Paris, 1905, Figure 61), the artist forms a more discrete part of the motif. The painting of a stately wedding procession in remarkably shabby and dull surroundings achieves a very strong social dimension through its oppositions. Among the greyish spectators of the wedding procession sits a man with his back towards the viewer. His shapeless hat is the same one that Arosenius usually portrayed himself wearing, and he blends

**Figure 58** *Toilette* (1905)

**Figure 61** *Paris Wedding* (Bröllop, Paris, 1905)

with the artist as well as the viewer through his position: just as the viewer of the artwork sees the scenery over the shoulder of the painter, the viewer as well as the painter see the scenery over the shoulder of the character with Arosenius' hat. Furthermore, while Arosenius regularly signed his works with his initials and year, as a rule he did not make his signature part of the scenery. In this painting, however, the signature is inscribed in one of the paving stones in the back street – the one right beside the character with Arosenius' hat, in yet another way blending the dimensions.[23]

---

[23] The painting might be connected to the circumstances in Paris, where Arosenius appears to have been interested in the Norwegian singer Gudrun Høyer-Ellefsen (employed by Arosenius as a fairy-tale princess), who at any rate was of fundamental importance to him but later married Axel Törneman (Asplund 1928, 82). No facial resemblances point in this direction, and the marriage as such took place far away from Arosenius in 1908.

**Figure 62** *Triumph of Venus* (Venus triumf, 1906)

In the painting *Triumph of Venus* (Venus triumf, 1906, Figure 62), Arosenius the same year proposed an entirely different procession in honour of love. Here, all sorts of people take part in the procession, from a jester via common people to an upper-class gentleman and what appears to be a bride. Only a few characters, including the pregnant Venus at the front, are painted in nuances which make them stand out from the crowd. One of those that stand out through colouring is the artist himself, entirely in black, dragging himself forward with a bottle in hand. He thus emerges as a not-too-felicitous worshipper not only of Venus, but also of Bacchus. While this character is in the foreground, the procession is observed by a spectator, viewing it from a balcony in the background. Sitting on the balcony, with his cheek supported by his hand in a relaxed, possibly amused and sympathetic stance, is the artist once again.[24] The woman holding a child inside the door behind him places him in his familial setting. This second staging of the artist in the same painting is distanced, in control, taking in the scenery which includes himself, perhaps in order to later use artistically – which can probably be seen, again, as an illustration of the command: you shall write/paint your life. While we have seen Arosenius portray himself doubly before, in *Those Beautiful Days*

---

[24] The doubling has been pointed out by Bing (*Ivar Arosenius 1878–1909* (1990)), who, however, understands the emotions of Arosenius on the balcony differently.

*Are Passed*, he now has developed one of the doublings into a viewer. (In a sketch for this work ([Figure 63]), there is no trace of an ambition to paint his own traits into the procession.)

Arosenius in this way paints himself into the diegesis of the scene but also creates a second diegetic level where he is removed from the actions – thus directing the viewer's perspective in two different ways (cf. Kemp 1998, 187). Significantly, this painting was composed at the same time as Arosenius initiated the shift from bohemian outsider to controlled artist and family father.

## 4.6 Staging the Artist's Home – and the Absent Self

After marrying, Arosenius and his wife settled in the apartment in Åby in 1906. Their daughter was born there in July, and a number of paintings came to present the family. About the same time, after a medical crisis, Arosenius started working with greater intensity and in larger formats than before, in an obvious will to establish a firmer position as a painter. This is when he painted *Inebriation* (Rus, 71 × 125 cm, 1906 [Figure 64]), which he considered to be his 'Museum Painting' (Fredlund 2009, 153, 143). The motif of drinking and sensuality/sexuality was not new in itself, but it was developed with much more care and with much more distance: the artist is in no way part of what is portrayed, but can be understood as the skilful composer of the motif. That is, Arosenius has left the Vangoghian paradigm but not the outsider motifs, rather like he in *Triumph of Venus* distanced himself from the bacchic carnival he had himself been part of.

In 1907, the family moved to a small house in Älvängen. It was very consciously furnished and decorated, and included the artist's studio. However, it differed from other artists' homes at the time, such as that of Carl Larsson, in that it was not at all ostentatious. The home contained many paintings, also on walls, doors and furniture, and was obviously furnished with the little daughter in mind – a great number of paintings portray her and the spouse in their home as it had been furnished and decorated (Fredlund 2009, 156–169). The artist's home thus was the stage where he presented himself and his works, and as such one of the Arosenius project's focal points on the Web and as an app.[25]

The artist's home in Älvängen thus effected a double staging: first, it was furnished analogously to the contemporary concepts and paintings of an artist's home – but in a distanced way, refraining from ostentation. Second, it provided the setting for a large number of paintings where the artist's home and family were staged for the canvas – also in analogy with the contemporary vogue for self-representation, but as we shall see, again in a distanced and independent way. The

---

[25] aroseniusarkivet.dh.gu.se/projekt/arosenius-i-alvangen; itunes.apple.com/us/app/dockhemmet/id1325606493?mt=8.

**Figure 65** *Portrait of the Artist's Wife* (Porträtt av konstnärens hustru, 1906)

staging of the previous home in Åby was less systematic, but already there the home had become the setting of, for example, *Portrait of the Artist's Wife* (Porträtt av konstnärens hustru, 1906, Figure 65). Not only was this very humble home realistically represented, but the artist's own paintings also already here came to form part of the staging of the motif. Included in the painting is at least the first image of *The Tale of the Six Princesses* (Sagan om de sex prinsessorna; Weibull 1988, 33), and the portrait of Karin Andersson is clearly recognizable.[26] This staging of the artist's actual surroundings was also incorporated in the self-portrait mentioned earlier, where he pictured himself before the mythologized landscape of Älvängen. The staging of the home coincides with Arosenius' energetic work to establish himself distinctly as a painter, making larger paintings and working more actively towards being exhibited and known – and paid.

In a number of other works, the artist stages himself through absence, in ways that draw attention to his not being viewed but instead viewing. From the moment his daughter was born, she became Arosenius' favourite model, and the home in Älvängen became the scene of many paintings. As Weibull points out, while joining the home and family focus, Arosenius seems to have distanced himself from the manner of Carl Larsson's self-stagings not least by *not*

[26] aroseniusarkivet.dh.gu.se/#/image/3956. A photograph of Arosenius sitting on the same couch in Åby, with partially the same paintings on the wall, is known (*Ivar Arosenius* 1988, 11). aroseniusarkivet.dh.gu.se/#/image/36.

placing himself in the scenery as the perfect family father (Weibull 1978, 130–135). Arosenius would not place himself in these family settings, but still could make himself noticeable through absence (Melander 2009, 39–41). Arosenius stages his absence.

Thus, a few family motifs belong to the previously treated instances of self-staging and self-pasting. There is at least one drawing of Arosenius and his daughter (1906, Figure 66), the loveliness of the scene balanced by the contrast between the father's happy smile and the daughter's crying, it appears. On closer inspection, it turns out that the loving father not only holds a crying child, but, in fact, innocently embraces a crying devil with horns and tail, much in the vein of *Antichrist*.[27] There are some family portraits including Arosenius, but converted into a mythological setting and thus rather being self-pastings: *Idyll* (Idyll, 1907 [Figure 67]) and *The Happy Family* (Den lyckliga familjen, 1908 [Figure 68]; Melander 2009, 38, 41).

However, in the home interiors with daughter and/or wife, Arosenius is remarkably absent. At the same time, his presence is underscored when Lillan plays with his hat or pipe (Weibull 1978, 135), or when a chair

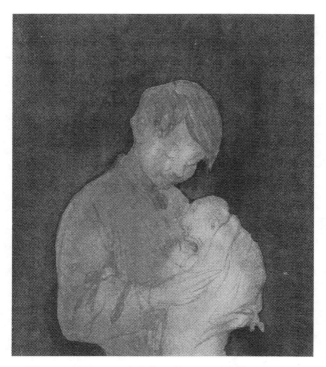

**Figure 66** *Ivar with Lillan* (Ivar med Lillan, 1906)

---

[27] These details were pointed out to me by Björn Fredlund.

stands empty as if he has just left the scene (*Madonna*, 1907, Figure 69; Melander 2009, 29). To these effects can be added that of the artist's own paintings hanging on the walls (Fredlund 2009, 168). Besides the just-mentioned *Portrait of the Artist's Wife, Lillan by the Door* (Lillan vid dörren, 1908, Figure 70) is one of the more illustrative examples. The paintings thus not only underline his presence in the room as family father, but also suggest his presence as artist, and so, in a sense, propose the same kind of meta-level artistic statement as in several of his self-portraits, but in a manner which more decisively blends life and art.

The effect of this negative staging is a considerable focus on the father, reinforcing the loving character of the motif in a way that corresponds to Petrarch's *Canzone* 126, 'Chiare, fresche', but by way of opposition. Petrarch conjured up the beloved from an environment where she was no longer, through his memories. Within the images, Arosenius conjures up the father's love by painting an environment where he is not. It is as if he has just left his place with his family to position himself on the other side of the easel, in order to paint

**Figure 69** *Madonna* (1907)

**Figure 70** *Lillan by the Door* (Lillan vid dörren, 1908)

them. The artist thus accentuates his withdrawal from viewed to viewer. This manoeuvre has distinct implications for the audience of his art.

The home and the family as a motif had been exploited not least by Carl Larsson, by whom Arosenius was influenced in a number of ways, although he does not seem to have wanted to be seen as influenced. The motif in all its variations appeared as an option for Arosenius through his marriage to Eva Adler and the birth of their daughter. Arosenius had from the beginning painted himself, his friends and his surroundings, but when he decided to achieve a decisive breakthrough, one distinct part of this was the exploitation of his own home, staging it for his own idiosyncratic version of the in-vogue focus on artists' homes. The artist had always invited biographical understanding of many of his works, but the late period's exploitation of the artist's home offered a new, much more intense invitation to understand him biographically. It seems that this very intense, and yet strategic, exploitation of the familial setting became a new driver for viewers and interpreters to understand his entire work in strongly biographical terms.

## 4.7 Staging the Viewer: Perspective

Not only inserting himself on different diegetic levels and thus directing the beholders' perspective in a wide range of ways (cf. Kemp 1998), Arosenius also explores the modes of perspective proper, not least when reaching the phase which would ensure his breakthrough. Taking the position of viewer instead of viewed, the artist invites his audience to partake more intensely. Even if he had placed himself in the scenery, the viewer of the painting would have seen the scenery from the painter's point of view, behind the easel or simply behind the canvas or paper he was using. However, when the scenery emphasizes the painter's absence as viewed, it also emphasizes his presence as viewer, and this strengthened presence is shared by the audience.

This manipulation of perspective was accompanied by other methods. Most markedly, Arosenius elaborated models to adopt the perspective of his daughter. So, during his last years, he produced a number of paintings where he incorporated the little child's perspective and emotional state. *Lillan by the Door*, already referred to, is one example. The most well-known one is *The Girl and the Candle* (Flickan och ljuset, 1907 [Figure 71]). Arosenius had been experimenting with perspective for a long time, perhaps, one might say, continuously. As Rossholm demonstrated, perspective is seminal in Arosenius' destabilizing the heroic genre when he forces the viewer to see human princesses through the perspective of the troll in *The Fairytale of the Six Princesses* (Sagan om de sex prinsessorna, 1905 [Figure 72]). By making a troll the identificatory character, Arosenius prevents the recipient from understanding it as a threat, and thus undermines the heroism of the troll-slaying hero (Rossholm 1978, 73–75). Other aspects of Arosenius' experiments with the perspective of Lillan and the home setting are thoroughly examined by Fredlund (2009, 137–195).

In exploring the perspective of the child, the artist did not orchestrate the scenery as if he were looking through the child's eyes. Instead, his principle of composition was to incorporate the figure of the child in the scenery and then project the child's perspective onto the surroundings, including the child herself. Through this manner of double exposure, as it were, the painter's perspective is not the same as the child's, but still blends with not only the perspective but also the emotional state of the child. As the viewer of the painting beholds everything through the eyes of the painter, the viewer as well partakes in the child's – and painter's – perspective and emotions. At the same time, through the elaborations in themselves, attention is drawn to the paintings' status as perspectival constructions and stagings of characters as well as emotions, even those of the non-visible artist. Just as he there makes the viewer see things the same way as the troll in *The Fairytale of the Six Princesses*, Arosenius through this method in his late paintings creates a very strong bind between himself and the viewer. This final method of staging his home, his daughter, himself and the viewer was most forceful.

Many of Arosenius' late works call to be understood as the result of an unreserved love, verging on obsession, for his child. She was a primary motif and he followed her through all her environments, often appropriating her perspective and reactions to the surrounding world. The Älvängen home was arranged with considerable consideration for the child (Fredlund 2009, 156–157). He made stories in images and words for her, the most renowned being *The Cat Journey* (Kattresan, posthumously published in 1909). Still, as Fredlund pointed out, the absolute engagement with the baby daughter, as it emerges in drawings and paintings, stands in contrast to how casually he mentions her in letters at the same time (Fredlund 2009, 148). It is well established that after a medical incident in 1906, just before the birth of his child, Arosenius started caring for his career and income in a new way, not only being more industrious, but also starting to work on a more monumental scale with large-size paintings. It is also well known that home, children and family had developed into a fruitful venue for contemporary artists. Even though Arosenius distanced himself from the ways artists such as Carl Larsson explored this venue, he certainly took part in this exploration. The choice of the small house in Älvängen as a home was not self-evident, and the artist devised every step in the furnishing of the house. The staging of the home as well as of Lillan in her surroundings (as of the mother) was congenial, and staging of emotions was a natural part of it – one which Arosenius developed in more forceful ways than his predecessors. This does not mean that the artist's emotions were not strong and sincere, but it makes it problematic to use his works as sources for his inner world and emotions.

## 5 Conclusions

Following the artist's self-stagings, it appears obvious that Arosenius inscribed himself from the beginning in the Vangoghian paradigm of the bohemian outsider of an artist which had emerged during the 1890s. This paradigm implied a shift in the ideal of art as harmonious towards disharmonious, of the genius from harmoniously successful to the incomprehensible or at least the artist disregarding success according to prevailing norms, from the normal to the abnormal, from excelling within the set rules to discarding them, and from evaluating the works, since they no longer followed norms, towards evaluating the person. Thus, life came to intermingle with art in intricate ways. However, at the moment Arosenius decided to strive to position himself and thus turn himself into cultural heritage, he very much abandoned the Vangoghian paradigm and reverted to an older notion of the genius, marked by harmony and balance. To be sure, Arosenius never endeavoured as hard as Carl Larsson, for example, to turn himself into cultural heritage, but the shift is significant. So, he not only started painting large, museal canvases, but also developed the image of the family man by exploring a sequence of motifs and techniques. This image inextricably employed the motif of house, household, wife and child, a context which was already established among artists but which Arosenius successfully developed into his very own. His developing of the fairy-tale genre equally consisted in refining existing traditions without bohemian rejection and a will to strongly provoke: it also connected to his new focus on the child and the child's view; having always used the world of fairy-tale in terms of motifs, with the new fairy-tale series he established a new kind of narrative. Arosenius continued to write/paint his life, but the new stage of his last years meant a stronger reworking of life and art than ever before. Although this repositioning left space for controversial motifs, such as *Inebriation*, it did so without the artist's role reverting to the Vangoghian paradigm. Rather, only as Arosenius abandoned the Vangoghian paradigm did he win substantial acclamation and breakthrough.

While this re-staging was acclaimed as a familial and simultaneously artistic consolidation and did result in the artist's general breakthrough, it appears that posterity was not ready to leave the Vangoghian image of Arosenius. The main reason appears to have been his premature death, which made the proximity to van Gogh even closer but also added an important layer, as van Gogh could never be interpreted in the light of a similarly impending death: there was no fatal disease to extrapolate meaning from. Posterity thus transcended the Vangoghian paradigm in aestheticizing Arosenius' death and making it artistically meaningful, a matrix for understanding his life and, not least, his art. This post-event perspective suggested understanding the artist's life and work as marked by the shadow of death, and of an anxiety resulting in strong polarization of contrasts. True, the artist had very elaborately explored opposites and contrasts, but the turn which caused his breakthrough was all about affirming life and harmony. It is difficult to ascertain to what extent Arosenius' early works were actually marked by his anxiety of an imminent death. He at least appears to have found very little use for that stance in his last years, and it was unknown to his wife, according to her own testimony.

Arosenius' two major roles, the early Vangoghian bohemian and the later, mature family man/artist, both directed focus on the artist's person. The later role at least focused on might rather than weakness, life rather than death. Posterity, however, appears to have projected death onto Arosenius also in his matured role. For instance, his focus on his daughter has been seen as a symbolism of life, implicating his own death also at this stage. How much of personal death and anguish resides in his works is impossible to answer, but obviously, life, person and work overlay each other. What can be concluded is that his use of blood, often connected to his disease, at an early stage consisted in an ingenious playfulness with stereotyped metaphors of love and heart; the grotesque murder scenes, often seen as expressions of despair at being left, are entirely consistent with themes current at the time in newspapers, literature and film after Jack the Ripper; his friend Ernst Spolén's descriptions of how he provoked fights as a kind of death wish are explained in earlier manuscripts by a wish to collect expressions and motifs for painting. In similar manner, the great attention he paid to his daughter certainly was artistic, but from letters appears not to have been caused by extraordinary personal emotions. Pragmatic considerations and artistic development, choice of techniques and motifs, certainly do not rule out biographic connections. The attempt here has rather been to map how this piece of cultural heritage has been modelled through the paintings in reception and to suggest alternative ways. Arosenius worked intensely with contrasts and emotions, and there is no way to isolate his works from his life.

The first part of this study thus presented the theoretical framework for a new way of staging the artist, in an archive which would gather representations of the artist's works, drafts, letters, sketches, etc. so as to make it possible to approach him from a number of different perspectives, letting the artefacts tell their story and contextualizing them in new ways. Seminal were the issues of mediation and agency, together with the concept 'staging', which, on the one hand, connects to the performativity of the artworks and thus to their agency and, on the other, provided the means for structuring the study into different aspects of what understandings of the artist the artefacts propose. The artist's works are mediations in the first instance, not only conveying outer and inner world, emotions, etc., but also an image of the artist. While they at one stage thus constituted his own – different – stagings of himself, after his death they came to be gathered, selected and ordered into repeatedly new stagings, mediated in new ways such as books, articles and exhibitions, or vanished into private homes.

The second part of this study was devoted to examining how the artist was staged in reception. The ways in which his biography governed the understanding of his works were examined, and the bohemian, Vangoghian paradigm was found to be a central structuring factor in the images of him. The Vangoghian paradigm was even more strengthened as the artist's haemophilia and knowledge of his imminent death were added to it, accentuating further the biographistic slant. The more tightly the works are inserted as parts of the matrix of the artist's biography, the smaller their agency is. The works offer other explanatory models when they are assembled in a manner which lets them make their statements on their own or in conjunction in new contexts.

The third and final part of the study was an attempt to retrace the statement of the artworks by re-ordering and re-collecting them – through new kinds of mediation – in a number of ways. This was done in a preliminary, explorative way, attempting to overhear the statements of the artefacts themselves, acknowledging the agency of the objects. The self-portraits proper gave instructions how to understand the artist in later years, while the bohemian Arosenius produced less statement-like, but still telling, renderings of himself. Paintings where traits of the artist were pasted onto characters addressed other issues of artistry, while self-stagings where the artist was viewed in different ways further developed the role of the artist. Yet other self-stagings turned the artist into viewer – and here the shift from the Vangoghian paradigm's outsider finds its most pregnant expression. In *Triumph of Venus* (Figure 62) the outsider and bohemian artist follows the bacchic train as before, but instead of being a character entirely within, the artist takes a perspective on himself and the scenery from above. At the same time, he starts writing museal works, presenting the bacchic and the venereal in a manner where the artist is entirely in control, distanced from but expert in his motifs. This change in staging of the artist is then developed further, as the motifs change both into saga series and into the painter's home, where not only the home, the wife and the daughter are ingeniously staged, but also the artist's staging as the invisible viewer and portrayer directs the perspective of the viewer of the painting itself, thus staging the audience of the paintings in a unique manner. This is the narrative related by the objects as they offer themselves in this particular filtering of the Arosenius Archive.

Previous stagings of Arosenius have in different ways formed part of the making of him into cultural heritage. The present staging – this study – does not renounce those forms of cultural heritage, but rather seeks to broaden the scope and widen the access. An interpretation can attempt to let the works govern the conclusions, and if this study has suggested some ways, it is the ambition of the Arosenius Archive portal to release the images for other ways of viewing, filtering and combining, letting one image lead the way to the other. So, it is hoped that through the agency of the digital medium, the agency of the works will be enhanced – as well as the agency of the audience, public as well as researchers. In this way, the artist's self-staging is expected to allow examination through the artefacts, rather than through the stagings made after his death. This study is a first attempt to use the infrastructure to invite the works of the artist to combine in new constellations and contexts, and suggest new interpretations. The tentative state of the study should be kept in mind: material will be added to the archive, metadata sets limits and calls for completing, new methods for sorting, filtering and contextualizing will be developed – this is very far from final knowledge.

# References

*Amateur/Eldsjäl: Variable Research Initiatives 1900 and 2000.* (2000). Gothenburg: Göteborgs Konstmuseum.

Arping, Å. (2014). Den estetiskt meningsfulla författardöden? Victoria Benedictssons självmord mellan tragedi och triumf. In Kristina Hermansson, Christian Lenemark and Cecilia Pettersson, eds., *Liv, lust och litteratur: Festskrift till Lisbeth Larsson.* Gothenburg: Makadam, pp. 55–63.

Asplund, K. (1928). *Ivar Arosenius.* Stockholm: Sveriges allmänna konstförening.

Austin, J. L. (1962). *How to Do Things with Words: The William James Lectures Delivered at Harvard University in 1955.* Oxford: Clarendon Press.

Benjamin, W. (1968). *Illuminations: Essays and Reflections.* Ed. and introd. Hannah Arendt, transl. Harry Zohn. New York: Schocken Books.

Bennett, T. (1995). *The Birth of the Museum: History, Theory, Politics.* London and New York: Routledge.

Bennett, T. (2018). *Museums, Power, Knowledge: Selected Essays.* London and New York: Routledge.

Bennett, T., Cameron, F., Dias, N., Dibley, B., Harrison, R., Jacknis, I. and McCarty, C. (2017). *Collecting, Ordering, Governing. Anthropology, Museums, and Liberal Government.* Durham, NC: Duke University Press.

Bjørnstad, K. (2001). *Jæger: En rekonstruksjon.* Oslo: Aschehoug.

Bjurström, P. (1978). Kring några bildidéer. In *Ivar Arosenius.* Stockholm: Nationalmuseum, pp. 15–66.

Bjurström, P. (1996). *Ivar Arosenius.* Stockholm: Cordia.

Blackman, L. (2016). Affect, Mediation and Subjectivity-as-Encounter: Finding the *Feeling* of the Foundling. *Journal of Curatorial Studies,* 5(1), pp. 33–55.

Bolter, J. D. and Grusin, R. (1999). *Remediation: Understanding New Media.* Cambridge, MA: MIT Press.

Bovenschen, S. (1976). Über die Frage: Gibt es eine 'weibliche' Ästhetik? In Gabriele Dietze, ed., *Die Überwindung der Sprachlosigkeit: Texte aus der neuen Frauenbewegung.* Darmstadt and Neuwied: Hermann Luchterhand Verlag (2. Aufl. 1981), pp. 82–115.

Bronfen, E. (1992). *Over Her Dead Body: Death, Femininity and the Aesthetic.* Manchester: Manchester University Press.

Codell, J. (2003). *The Victorian Artist: Artists' Lifewritings in Britain, ca. 1870–1910.* Cambridge: Cambridge University Press.

Epstein, W. H. ed. (1991). *Contesting the Subject: Essays in the Postmodern Theory and Practice of Biography and Biographical Criticism.* West Lafayette, IN: Purdue University Press.

Fosli, H. (1994). *Kristianiabohemen: Byen, miljøet, menneska.* Oslo: Det Norske Samlaget.

Fredlund, B. (2009). *Ivar Arosenius.* Stockholm: Signum.

Gram, M. (1996). Karl Wåhlins konstsyn. *Konsthistorisk tidskrift / Journal of Art History*, 65(4), 253–278.

Grinell, K. and Portin, F. (unpublished). *The Diplomatic Museum.*

Guercio, G. (2006). *Art as Existence: The Artist's Monograph and Its Project.* Cambridge, MA and London: MIT Press.

Guggenheim, M. (2009). Building Memory: Architecture, Networks and Users. *Memory Studies*, 2, 39–53.

Harrison, R. (2013). Reassembling Ethnographic Museum Collections. In Rodney Harrison, Sarah Byrne and Anne Clarke, eds., *Reassembling the Collection: Ethnographic Museums and Indigenous Agency.* Santa Fe, NM: School for Advanced Research Press, pp. 3–35.

Harvey, D. C. (2008). The History of Heritage. In Brian Graham and Peter Howard, eds., *The Ashgate Research Companion to Heritage and Identity.* Aldershot: Ashgate, pp. 19–36.

Haynes, D. J. (1997). *The Vocation of the Artist.* Cambridge: Cambridge University Press.

Heinich, N. (1996). *The Glory of Van Gogh: An Anthropology of Admiration*, transl. Paul Leduc Browne. Princeton, NJ: Princeton University Press.

Hermansson, G. (2010). *Lyksalighedens øer: Møder mellem poesi, religion og erotik i dansk og svensk romantik.* Gothenburg: Makadam.

Hermansson, G. (2020). Lystmord, krig og ekspressionisme. Dansk ekspressionisme og tysk avantgardekunst efter Første Verdenskrig. In Torben Jelsbak and Anna Sandberg, eds., *Dansk-tyske krige. Kulturliv og kulturkampe.* Copenhagen: Copenhagen University Press, pp. 245–270.

Hjern, K. (1961). *Ivar Arosenius och hans stad*, Uppsala: Almqvist & Wiksell.

Huhtamo, E. and Parikka, J. (2011). Introduction: An Archaeology of Media Archaeology. In E. Huhtamo and J. Parikka, eds., *Media Archaeology: Approaches, Applications, and Implications.* Berkeley, CA: University of California Press, pp. 1–21.

*Ivar Arosenius.* (1978). Stockholm: Nationalmuseum. (Per Bjurström, Margaretha Rossholm, Nina Weibull)

*Ivar Arosenius.* (1988). Borås: Borås Konstmuseum. (Tomas Lindh, Nina Weibull, Kristina and Carl-Magnus Stolt, Gunnel Enby)

*Ivar Arosenius.* (2005). *Akvareller/Watercolours.* Skärhamn: Nordiska akvarellmuseet. (Bera Nordal, Joanna Persman)

*Ivar Arosenius. 1879–1909.* (1958). Gothenburg: Göteborgs Konstmuseum. (Alfred Westholm, Sven Sandström)

*Ivar Arosenius. 1878–1909.* (1979). *Bilder und Graphik.* Karlsruhe: Museumsgesellschaft Ettlingen. (Björn Fredlund)

*Ivar Arosenius. 1878–1909.* (1990). København: Storm P.-museet. (Jens Bing)

*Ivar Arosenius: Minnesutställning.* (1926). Stockholm: P.A. Norstedt. (Gunnar Wengström)

*Ivar Arosenius Sagor. Femtiosex bilder.* (1939). Ed. and introd. A. L. Romdahl, Stockholm.

Jaensson, K. (1944). Bohemen och målaren. *Konstrevy,* 20(4), 147–154.

Jansson, M. (2014). *Poetens blick: Ekfras i svensk lyrik.* Stockholm/Höör: Brutus Östlings Bokförlag Symposion.

*Julstämning. 50-årsminnet av Ivar Arosenius.* (1958). Göteborg: Julstämnings förlag.

Kemp, W. (1998). The Work of Art and Its Beholder: The Methodology of the Aesthetic of Reception. In Mark A. Cheetham, ed., *The Subjects of Art History: Historical Objects in Contemporary Perspectives.* Cambridge: Cambridge University Press, pp. 180–196.

Lagerlöw-Sandell, S., Spolén, E., Linden-Buchman, A, Sandström, S. and Wahlström, F. (1956). *Ivar Arosenius. Ole Kruse. Gerhard Henning. Minnesbilder.* Gothenburg: Rundqvist.

Larsson, L. (2007). Biografins återkomster. In Henrik Rosengren and Johan Östling, eds., *Med livet som insats: Biografin som humanistisk genre.* Lund: Sekel, pp. 51–59.

Larsson, L. (2008). *Hennes döda kropp: Victoria Benedictssons arkiv och författarskap.* Stockholm: Weyler.

Latour, B. (1993). *We Have Never Been Modern,* transl. Catherine Porter. Cambridge, MA: Harvard University Press.

Latour, B. (1999). *Pandora's Hope.* Essays on the Reality of Science Studies. Cambridge, MA: Harvard University Press.

Latour, B. (2005). *Reassembling the Social: An Introduction to Actor-Network-Theory.* Oxford: Oxford University Press.

Latour, B. and Lowe, A. (2011). The Migration of the Aura, or How to Explore the Original through Its Facsimiles. In T. Bartscherer and R. Coover, eds., *Switching Codes: Thinking through Digital Technology in the Humanities and the Arts.* Chicago, IL: University of Chicago Press, pp. 275–297.

Liepe, L. (2018). *A Case for the Middle Ages: The Public Display of Medieval Church Art in Sweden 1847–1943*. Stockholm: Kungl. Vitterhets Historie och Antikvitets Akademien.

Lundbo Levy, J. (1980). *Dobbeltblikket: om at beskrive kvinder. Ideologi og æstetik i Victoria Benedictssons forfatterskab.* Copenhagen: Tiderne skifter.

Mankell, B. (2003). *Självporträtt: En bildanalytisk studie i svensk 1900-talskonst.* Gothenburg: Acta Universitatis Gothoburgensis.

Melander, S. (2009). *Ivar Arosenius i Älvängen. Den lyckliga familjen.* Gothenburg: B4Press.

Moi, T. (1994). *Simone de Beauvoir: The Making of an Intellectual Woman.* Oxford: Blackwell.

Montgomery, K. (1986). Ole Kruse i sekelskiftets Göteborg: Bröderna och Brödrarummet. *Konsthistoriska studier*, 9, 125–134.

Nordström, L. (2000). *Första boken om Ivar Arosenius*. Stockholm: Almqvist & Wiksell.

Olsson, T. (1989). Det estetiskt meningsfulla författarlivet – en litteraturvetenskaplig tankefigur. *Samlaren: Tidskrift för svensk litteraturvetenskaplig forskning*, 110, 27–37.

Parikka, J. (2013). Afterword: Cultural Techniques and Media Studies. *Theory Culture & Society*, 30, 147–159.

Persman, J. (2005). 'Konst är inte så konstigt' – akvarellkonstnären Ivar Arosenius. In *Ivar Arosenius: Akvareller/Watercolours*. Skärhamn: Nordiska akvarellmuseet, pp. 9–44.

Possing, B. (2015). *Ind i biografien*. Copenhagen: Gyldendal.

Rees Leahy, H. (2009). Assembling Art, Constructing Heritage. *Journal of Cultural Economy*, 2(1–2), 135–149.

Roberts, M. (1990). *Gothic Immortals: The Fiction of the Brotherhood of the Rosy Cross*. London: Routledge.

Romdahl, A. (1909). *Ivar Arosenius: Tjugonio bilder i färg*. Gothenburg: Åhlén & Åkerlund.

Romdahl, A. (1944). *Ivar Arosenius*. Gothenburg: Bokkonst.

Rossholm, M. (1978). Arosenius' sagor. In *Ivar Arosenius*. Stockholm: Nationalmuseum, pp. 67–123.

Rossholm Lagerlöf, M. (2007). *Inlevelse och vetenskap – om tolkning av bildkonst*. Stockholm: Atlantis.

Sandström, S. (1959). *Ivar Arosenius: Hans konst och liv*. Stockholm: Albert Bonniers förlag.

Sandström, S. (1995). Ivar Arosenius – människa, attityd och tidsstil. In I. Bergström, A. Nordin, L. Stackell and J. Werner, eds., *Det skapande jaget: Konsthistoriska texter tillägnade Maj-Britt Wadell*, Gothenburg: Konstvetenskapliga institutionen, pp. 43–50.

Silberman, N. (2008). Chasing the Unicorn? The Quest for 'Essence' in Digital Heritage. In Y. Kalay, T. Kvan and J. Affleck, eds., *Cultural Heritage and New Media*. London: Routledge, pp. 81–91.

Smith, L. (2006). *Uses of Heritage*. New York: Routledge.

Soussloff, C. M. (1997). *The Absolute Artist: The Historiography of a Concept*. Minneapolis, MN: University of Minneapolis Press.

Spolén, E. (1956). Med Ivar Arosenius i Värmland. Glimtar från gemensamma upplevelser sommaren 1902. In S. Lagerlöw-Sandell, E. Spolén, A. Linden-Buchman, S. Sandström and F. Wahlström, eds., *Ivar Arosenius. Ole Kruse. Gerhard Henning. Minnesbilder*. Gothenburg: Rundqvist, pp. 47–55.

Spolén, E. (1963). *Ivar Arosenius: En minnesbild*, Stockholm: Norstedt.

Stolt, K. and Stolt, C.-M. (1988). Ivar Arosenius och blödarsjukdomen. In *Ivar Arosenius*. Borås: Borås Konstmuseum, pp. 49–59.

Svärdström, S. (1944). *Dalmålningar. Samlade och kommenterade av Svante Svärdström*. Stockholm: Albert Bonniers förlag.

Wåhlin, K. (1909). Svenska humorister. *Stockholms Dagblad*, 20 December 1909 (aroseniusarkivet.dh.gu.se/#/image/2566).

Walsh, P. (2007). Rise and Fall of the Post-Photographic Museum. In Fiona Cameron and Sarah Kenderdine, eds., *Theorizing Digital Cultural Heritage: A Critical Discourse*. Cambridge, MA: MIT Press, pp. 19–34.

Weibull, N. (1978). Lillans värld. In *Ivar Arosenius*, Stockholm: Nationalmuseum, pp. 125–152.

Weibull, N. (1988). Med kvinnligheten i centrum. In *Ivar Arosenius*. Borås: Borås Konstmuseum, pp. 17–36.

Wengström, G. (1926). Introduction. *Ivar Arosenius: Minnesutställning*. Stockholm: P.A. Norstedt & söner, pp. v–xi.

Westin, J. (2012). Towards a Vocabulary of Limitations: The Translation of a Painted Goddess into a Symbol of Classical Education. *The International Journal of Heritage Studies*, 1, 18–32. doi.org/10.1080/13527258 .2011.590818.

Wittkower, R. and Wittkower, M. (1963). *Born Under Saturn: The Character and Conduct of Artists – A Documented History from Antiquity to the French Revolution*. London: Weidenfeld and Nicolson.

# Acknowledgements

I would like to express my gratitude for valuable comments and help to Birte Bruchmüller, Annika Bünz, Dick Claésson, Alexandra Fried, Alexandra Herlitz, Astrid von Rosen, Christine Sjöberg, Astrid Torstensson, Karin Wagner and Jonathan Westin, as well as the two peer reviewers.

# Cambridge Elements ☰

# Critical Heritage Studies

Kristian Kristiansen
*University of Gothenburg*

Michael Rowlands
*UCL*

Francis Nyamnjoh
*University of Cape Town*

Astrid Swenson
*Bath University*

Shu-Li Wang
*Academia Sinica*

Ola Wetterberg
*University of Gothenburg*

## About the Series

This series focuses on the recently established field of Critical Heritage Studies. Interdisciplinary in character, it brings together contributions from experts working in a range of fields, including cultural management, anthropology, archaeology, politics, and law. The series will include volumes that demonstrate the impact of contemporary theoretical discourses on heritage found throughout the world, raising awareness of the acute relevance of critically analysing and understanding the way heritage is used today to form new futures.

**Cambridge Elements** ≡

# Critical Heritage Studies

---

Printed in the United States
by Baker & Taylor Publisher Services